Praise for *Middle Lea* *for 21st Century Sc*

The strength of this book lies in the honest reflections draws upon his own experience in middle and senior lea

Covering a range of important topics – from the value of interpersonal skills, to preparation for further promotion and senior leadership – Bill also explores practical details and relevant management theory from the world of education and wider business. He carefully selects some useful insights from recent research and urges the reader to reflect on their own practice in each area.

Middle Leadership for 21st Century Schools will be very useful for middle leaders looking to research leadership further, whilst the references to further reading will also be invaluable to the aspiring MA student of leadership.

> Caroline Bentley-Davies, middle leadership expert
> and author of *How to Be an Amazing Middle Leader*

Occasionally, one reads a book that can make a profound difference to the success of an individual or organisation. *Middle Leadership for 21st Century Schools* is such a book. It is an enlightening, thought-provoking text that provides a new perspective on this vital area of school leadership and a road map for modern and effective practice. A must-read.

> Chris Griffiths, CEO, OpenGenius Ltd, innovation expert
> and bestselling co-author of *The Creative Thinking Handbook*

Bill's book highlights the importance and relevance of the changing nature of middle leadership in schools, effectively guiding the reader through the demands of the role. It encourages established leaders to reflect on and refine their practice, and is both a "bible" for the aspiring middle leader and a useful resource to support school leadership course requirements and projects.

> Lynn Seal, Head of School, Kennington CE Academy

Middle Leadership for 21st Century Schools is a well-written, well-referenced book offering great insights for those working in and around the often overlooked but crucial area of middle leadership.

> Richard Bradley, Managing Director, Master Trainer Institute

Middle Leadership for 21st Century Schools is an extremely inspiring and motivational book which explores fundamental concepts relating to middle leadership and its place in an educational landscape which has transformed dramatically over the years.

The useful strategies, case study quotes from a range of teachers and Bill's honesty in sharing his personal experiences make this book relatable to all, seamlessly linking the theory of leadership to everyday classroom experience. The use of reflective questions and evaluations also makes the book thought-provoking as well as informative, and it when we reflect on and relate to our own practice that we truly see Bill's intentions in driving effective and committed middle leadership within schools. Furthermore, his suggestions on how to overcome barriers in order to lead change are successful in helping us to explore leadership through the eyes of every teacher.

Without a doubt, this is a very insightful and enlightening book – and I highly recommend it to all aspiring and practising middle leaders in education.

Jenny Wilkinson, teacher and middle leader, Church of the Ascension Primary School

Middle Leadership for 21st Century Schools is a most timely publication: a book that gets to the heart of leadership through a clear and substantiated narrative accessible to all.

It is an informed and well-written text that helps readers get past the "what" of leadership by succinctly and eloquently exploring the "why". Bill Lowe draws from his broad professional experience to illustrate key ideas and concepts, whilst constantly reinforcing these with a wide variety of academic references, and shares a wealth of advice and commentary on what constitutes professional practice. He also provides a range of practical activities and accompanying reflections that guide the reader through the fundamental differences between managers and leaders. Importantly, he also covers system leadership – which is so pertinent considering the shifting educational landscape of school leadership with the emergence of alliances and multi-academy trusts.

Quite simply, *Middle Leadership for 21st Century Schools* is a vital resource for all who aspire to lead and for all who do lead.

Mark Chidler, PGCE Course Coordinator, Newman University, Birmingham

Middle Leadership for 21st Century Schools delivers a superb lesson in school leadership that puts the spotlight on understanding and developing people. Bill provides established and aspiring middle leaders with a wealth of practical actions to help them expand their skill set, become more confident in their role and address modern challenges in teaching practice.

The go-to guide for all middle leaders looking to drive positive change within their schools.

Melina Costi, co-author of *The Positive Leader* and *The Creative Thinking Handbook*

Bill Lowe

Middle Leadership
for 21st Century Schools

From Compliance to Commitment

Crown House Publishing Limited
www.crownhouse.co.uk

First published by
Crown House Publishing
Crown Buildings, Bancyfelin, Carmarthen, Wales, SA33 5ND, UK
www.crownhouse.co.uk

and

Crown House Publishing Company LLC
PO Box 2223, Williston, VT 05495, USA
www.crownhousepublishing.com

First published 2019.

Cover image © denis_pc – fotolia.com.

Quotes from Ofsted and Department for Education documents used in this publication
have been approved under an Open Government Licence. Please see: http://www.
nationalarchives.gov.uk/doc/open-government-licence/version/3/.

British Library of Cataloguing-in-Publication Data
A catalogue entry for this book is available from the British Library.

Print ISBN 978-178583434-9
Mobi ISBN 978-178583473-8
ePub ISBN 978-178583474-5
ePDF ISBN 978-178583475-2

LCCN 2019951610

Printed in the UK by
TJ International, Padstow, Cornwall

Preface

An inspiration for writing this book comes from Robert Greene talking on Tom Bilyeu's *Impact Theory* YouTube channel. Robert speaks of how he coaches and advises some of the most famous, powerful and influential people in the world. They invite him to help them.

He states that: "The number one problem they have is their inability to understand the people they are dealing with." Robert explains how they hire people who are experts in their field – technically brilliant – but who don't understand the basics of the people around them. He argues that the primary skill in life should be "understanding people" (quoted in Bilyeu, 2018).

21st century leadership in schools is in danger of overlooking this primary skill. There are many places where you can find the tools for leadership and management that will make you technically proficient. But there is a lot more to it than that.

Acknowledgements

My thanks go to all the people I've worked with over the years. I thank them for the patience they have shown when I've asked them, again and again, for their comments on workplace issues.

I have always believed in the honesty of my colleagues and that there is no better source of information than the people doing the job. I have changed their names when quoting their words in this book. Although some were happy to be named, others were reluctant, and I understand this.

My sincere thanks go to the team at Crown House Publishing for their friendly and professional way of dealing with this publication. Writing this book has been a real learning experience and, in particular, I'd like to thank copy-editors Emma Tuck and Louise Penny for their guidance and patience.

Contents

Introduction

Welcome to leadership

Middle leadership is one of the hardest roles in any workplace. In your early days, you realise that you are now not only responsible for the teaching that goes on in your classroom, but also for other people and the way they teach in their classrooms. Get it right and the positive impact you will have on a lot of young people's learning is difficult to calculate. Get it wrong and the damage done will be all too easy to see.

It soon becomes evident that your leadership role gives you wider influence and responsibility. Now your work is not only centred around your class but also around the colleagues who you lead. As John Maxwell (2013) puts it: "Successful people know what they're good at. Successful leaders know what other people are good at."

It is one of the toughest jobs because middle leadership is usually the first step on the leadership ladder. You will be doing many things for the first time and you will have a lot of eyes on you. Paul Irvine and Mark Brundrett (2016: 86) state, "Those taking on leadership roles in schools require a different skills set to that of the classroom teacher." At middle leader level, you will be adding to your skill set as the demands of your role increase. Learn the leadership fundamentals at this stage and they will hold up through the levels of authority you take on as you make your way up the career ladder. The strategies that you apply as a middle leader will be part of your work in more senior positions, so it makes sense to have a strong understanding from the outset. If you give yourself some solid foundations, the rest of your leadership career will be easier to build.

Why do it?

Billions of words have been written and spoken about leadership, but, in particular, those of Professor Rosabeth Moss Kanter (2013) from Harvard University Business School stand out. "What are you working on today?" she was asked by a colleague one morning.

She replied that she was trying to: "Provide other people with the tools for making the world a better place, by giving them leadership skills."

I can't think of a better reason for going into leadership.

Why did I write this book?

I believe that if you are not shown the right way to teach a subject, you will teach it in the same way that you were taught it. As a student teacher, I had no instruction in how to teach art. So when I then had to teach the subject to a class of 8-year-olds, my lessons were very similar to the ones I experienced when I was that age. My concern is that if any of those 8-year-olds then went on to train as teachers in adulthood, and had no training in art teaching, they would teach art as I had taught it to them. In effect, the same teaching I'd had decades ago.

I see no difference with leadership. This is recognised by Paul Irvine and Mark Brundrett (2016), who suggest that a lot of teachers who take on middle leadership roles don't have the right training to start with and then lack a reasonable level of development support. If you do not have any guidance or understanding of what makes a good leader, then you will simply lead in the way that you have been led. This isn't to say that you haven't had great leaders, or lack the ability to emulate their practice to great effect, but what if the leadership you have had was not that effective? What if it was outdated? And what about having a strong understanding of the theories so that you can adapt them by stamping your own personality?

Simon Sinek (2016) talks about how a lot of current business leadership practice is based on the world as it was in the late 1980s and 1990s. It is now out of date, but people still persist. It is the same in some of our schools: a lot of leadership delivery does not fit the new way of doing things. We need to be aware that school structures have changed. Funding streams and accountability levels are unrecognisable in some instances – for example, the increase in delegated leadership across several schools. This might have been caused by budgetary influences or a politically motivated reorganisation of groupings of schools, but there are far fewer schools working in isolation than there were a decade ago. The growth of this "system leadership" model continues at quite a pace.

As we move deeper into the 21st century, I think that the *how* of leadership will become more of an area for development than the *what*. In the same way that Sinek argues that people are more important than money (treat the former well and the latter will follow), I see schools having to understand that people come first and test results second. Treat your colleagues well and lead them with compassion and empathy, and the exam results will follow.

In my travels, I've noticed the start of a swing away from particular strategies that have had a demonstrable impact on workload. Things that were deemed to be "best practice" last year are now seen as undesirable by some; but not everyone. This is why *how* we lead is so important. Strategies for how to lead can be applied to any model. The message is clear: leadership at all levels needs to move forward to accommodate the how. It is my hope that this book will help to address this need.

The book will introduce you to a range of useful strategies and the thinking that underpins them. Well-established leadership and management ideas are identified, alongside powerful strategies that work in the modern education world. References are made to some influential leadership experts, but this book goes beyond that. Importantly, it uses your own experiences of being a leader and being led to illustrate key points so that the theories can be seen in practice.

My aim is to get past the "what" of leadership in order to look at the details of the "how". Most schools have a hierarchy: some are less tiered and less formal than others, but nonetheless, you'll still be part of an authority ranking system. It took me a while to come up with titles for people within this framework. I don't feel particularly comfortable with individuals who are too full of their own self-importance. This has always made it difficult for me to think of a term for those who are beneath me in the hierarchy. "Subordinates" sounds like you think of these people as lesser humans than you. "Followers" makes it sound like some kind of cult, or as if you like to be defined by the size of your Twitter audience. These people are colleagues who you have been empowered to lead, so we'll call them "led colleagues" or "colleagues who you lead".

An important aspect of the book is its consideration of leadership training. We need to think about the differences in approaches.

- **Transmission leadership training:** the provision of training around techniques and procedures that need to be mastered.
- **Development learning leadership training:** leadership development should identify and understand the tensions and difficulties that are encountered as everyday work is carried out.

In *Collaborative School Leadership,* Philip Woods and Amanda Roberts (2018) argue effectively that a development learning approach to leadership is important. This does not reject the traditional transmission approach but helps to build on it.

This idea is backed up by the Center for Creative Leadership (CCL). On their website, they refer to the 70-20-10 rule of leadership training and development: 70% is learning on the job, but that needs to include some challenging projects, 20% is learning from other people and 10% is learning from training courses.[1] CCL believes that the 10% category will support, clarify and boost the remaining 90%. They are keen to point out

---

1 See https://www.ccl.org/articles/leading-effectively-articles/70-20-10-rule/.

that experiential practice needs to be built into any leadership training course. That way, we help leaders to not just perform better in their role but to be better learners as well. They call it the "amplifier effect".

The act of reflecting on practice and experience is built into this book. I want you to consider how things have been for you as a leader and as someone who is being led by senior colleagues. Being "on the receiving end", as it were, is a powerful learning experience. There are chances for you to reflect on things that you have seen, been subjected to and experienced first-hand. These are the *current experience reflection* activities. These are in bullet lists or table form. It is important to give yourself time to think about how things look in your present job. You will also have opportunities to think about how you might have done things differently and how you will approach things in the future. These are the *honest reflection* boxes. You might want to use a notebook so you can copy and complete the tables and honest reflection questions as you go along. Indeed, I hope that you will fully exploit these activities by starting a reflection journal of your own, the basis of which can be the tasks that we'll work through in this book. Doing this will let you develop your thoughts in a structure that suits you. You will not be constrained by a rigid, tick-box layout. Use it as a working document to take with you on your voyage through leadership. Think about a digital approach which would allow you to include audio/video files of chats with colleagues and evidence of your achievements.

The book hasn't been written to a formula, so don't expect the same number of reflection activities in each chapter. They have been included where they occur naturally, not forced. Consider revisiting the activities at different points in the future. This will give you the opportunity to reflect on how your understanding of your role is developing. It can be very enlightening to look back at opinions and beliefs that you used to have and see if experience has changed you in any way. Keeping a journal works for a lot of us. When I look back at my first months of headship, I wonder how I managed to last more than a term!

To get the most from the reflective activities, endeavour to ask other people about their perspectives. For this you'll need a critical friend and a developing network of leaders who you can contact. This approach is becoming established in modern leadership training. Mihnea Moldoveanu and Das Narayandas (2019) suggest that traditional leadership development strategies are not addressing the issues that leaders and their organisations face. Amongst the reasons they put forward for this are:

- Trainers not offering development in the soft skills required to be an effective leader.
- It is hard to apply "classroom learning" to the real world.

The rapid development of digital communication means that you don't have to rely on face-to-face discussions. You can develop your own personal learning cloud (PLC) and learn from both colleagues who you lead and other leaders. As Moldoveanu and Narayandas illustrate, this vehicle for leadership development is personal, social and entirely contextual. Reid Hoffman et al. (2019) add weight to this by saying that we should "Learn from people, not classes". They see the PLC as a way of keeping pace with changes and trends in an affordable way that avoids disruption. You can use this book to start this learning strategy. Try sharing your experiences and thoughts, prompted by this book, with experienced peers and more senior leaders through communication platforms like Zoom, Skype or FaceTime. You can take this further by using PLC tools such as Rackspace and KloudLearn. Productivity apps like Ayoa can be used for this as well.

Another aim of this book is to encourage you to think about how you'd approach certain issues at a middle management level, and how you'd change your practice if approaching them at a more senior level. This will give you experience which will be helpful if you become a senior leader. Dealing with conflict is a good example of this. Along with giving you techniques and procedures, I hope to uncover the possible tensions and difficulties that you might encounter. Being aware of these should help you to think about how problems can be turned around into leadership successes.

Leadership training should be an entitlement, but in the UK alone there are several different models and routes, which can confuse matters. For example, whilst in England (with its now non-mandatory National Professional Qualification for Headship (NPQH)) things are becoming more fragmented, with a lot of different providers looking to recruit candidates onto their courses, in Scotland they have an Into Headship qualification that will be mandatory for new head teachers from 2020.[2] Northern Ireland appears to be following the Scottish model. In Wales, one of the National Academy for Educational Leadership's objectives for 2018–2021 is to 'contribute to the reform and refocussing of the NPQH programme'.[3]

What this book is not intended to do is to give detailed advice on things like how to run a budget, write a whole-school policy or plan a subject-specific scheme of work. These are about the what, not the how. There are excellent resources that you can use for advice, and I can't think of a school that hasn't got its own documents in place.

Whilst writing this book, I was often concerned about including advice that seems too basic and perhaps patronising. However, having spoken with several teachers who are new to middle leadership, it became apparent that a lot of them had not had any

---

2 See https://www.scelscotland.org.uk/what-we-offer/into-headship/.
3 See http://nael.cymru/wp-content/uploads/2019/07/national-academy-for-educational-leadership-remit-letter-2018-2021.pdf.

leadership training. They were learning from day-to-day experience and making a lot of things up as they went along. They were low on confidence and, in some cases, this was exploited by colleagues. Therefore, if you think I'm occasionally stating the blindingly obvious, forgive me and appreciate that there will be some readers who will find it useful.

Those involved in leadership training agree that training should be ongoing. I hope that you use this book as a developmental tool at different stages of your leadership career.

What is middle leadership?

Schools can call the different positions in their hierarchies anything they like. Generally, you find senior leadership teams (SLTs) made up of deputy and assistant head teachers who report to the head teacher or principal. Anything below that is seen as middle leadership. This isn't like the definition and role of middle leaders in the corporate world, where middle leaders can be national sales managers or senior marketing executives. They might even be directors or vice-presidents. In some sectors, middle leaders can be very senior.

Basically, if you have someone else above and below you in the hierarchy, you are a middle leader. It is logical. In schools, the middle leadership layer tends to be comprised of subject leaders, heads of department and phase leaders. In some schools, key stage leaders can fall into this category, whilst in others they are part of the SLT. It is a very fluid picture.

Is it seen as an important role?

As a profession, we are good at being modest. "I'm only a class teacher" is something you'll hear a lot. It is the same with middle leaders. You are not "only a middle leader". You play an important role in the school. People with outside influence certainly know the vital part that middle leaders play.

I read in a 2018 Ofsted school inspection report that although the middle leaders in the school were being held to account by their senior leaders, they were not impacting on their own led colleagues. The school was judged as requiring improvement, suggesting that Ofsted, for one, recognise the significance of the position.

The challenges of middle leadership

As you work through this book, it is worth considering that the same types of challenge can affect the SLT layer all too often. Being aware of these issues now will help you to address them at a more senior level, as you will be prepared.

Middle leaders in 21st century schools have to be promoters and defenders of their subject or phase team. Examples of this could be fighting for your subject's timetable allocation, the rooms that your colleagues are given to teach in or your allocation of teaching assistants (TAs). In my experience, it is often the leaders of non-core subjects who have a fight on their hands with these issues. At the same time, the middle leader should be responsible for reporting their team members' concerns to senior leaders in a way that represents how the team feels.

People in this position have to lead colleagues to perform at a high level both in the classroom and outside of it. Monitoring team members' performance is a middle leader's responsibility and the outcomes of this also come into the remit. Who needs support and training? Who needs to be encouraged to take a leading role? What are the possible repercussions if we get it wrong? By asking these questions, a middle leader is looking for ways to develop the team. Improving your team's impact is a fundamental part of the job.

More often than not, middle leaders have to apply ways of working imposed by the SLT. We will see in later chapters how middle leaders can be caught between different factions, each with their own expectations. Middle leaders often have to deliver a message that might not be theirs, yet they will be in the firing line. They can be pushed and pulled in all directions.

You must be clear in your mind from the start: you will not be able to please everyone all the time. As newspaperman Herbert Bayard Swope reportedly observed: "I cannot give you the formula for success, but I can give you the formula for failure, which is: Try to please everybody."[4] Once you accept that, things will be easier. However, you must make sure that you know where your loyalties lie. This requires a good deal of self-awareness and the ability to stick to what you believe. We like to teach our students about resilience: you need to have it in large quantities.

Above all, buy into the learning development model – by which I mean, learn from your experiences and keep a record of what you do.

I wish you the very best of luck.

---

4 Quoted at: https://spartacus-educational.com/USAswope.htm.

Chapter 1

Leadership and Management: Some Definitions

People want to know what accounts for good leadership and how to become good leaders. Despite this strong interest in leadership, there are very few books that clearly describe the complexities of practicing leadership.

Peter Northouse (2015)

By the end of this chapter, you will have a clear idea of the general differences between leadership and management, as well as an appreciation of why you need to have both sets of skills. There are many books and training courses on leadership styles in existence. Here is not the place to spend too much time on these theories, but I hope this chapter will encourage you to find out more.

Some schools have SLTs whilst others have senior management teams (SMTs). Is there any difference? Probably not. In school, we are not as likely to have managers and leaders in two distinct groups, as they might be in the corporate world. Yes, we have business managers and timetable managers but, in general, middle leaders need to be both leader and manager at the same time. Think of leadership and management as two different sets of *skills*. Whether you are called a middle leader or a middle manager, you will need to have both leadership skills and management skills.

The differences between leadership and management

It is very common for individuals to be better at one skill set than the other. As we look at the characteristics of both, perhaps you will be able to identify yourself as having stronger elements in one area. Are you more of a leader or more of a manager? Perhaps you have a good balance of each.

In general terms:

▪ *Leadership* is about having an idea of what you want and how to get it. You know what you want to achieve and come up with new ideas about how to get there.

Good leaders are often innovators. You need people like this in order to move the school forward.

◼ *Management* is about the processes, structures and procedures that are needed to make things happen.

Those of us who are more management-oriented tend to like a process that is stable and will produce quick results. Strong managers will put monitoring and evaluation time-tables in place with meetings and feedback sessions arranged at suitable intervals.

It is clear to see that if you are fortunate enough to have both sets of skills, you will be a very effective head of department or key stage.

Although this is only a brief introduction to the differences, how do you see yourself?

Current experience reflection activity	
	Examples of why
I am a more natural leader.	
I am a more natural manager.	

What do they look like?

It is important to have a clear understanding of whether you need to be in leadership mode or management mode for a particular task. From the outset, identify your strengths and weaknesses, and ask to have these added to your performance management development plan. A common criticism of new leaders is their lack of self-awareness. I recognise this. As a new head of department, I was keen to publish timetables and provide clear structures, rules and regulations relating to my subject area. All I was doing was managing what was already in place. There was no vision or plan for developing my area. In fact, no leadership. Avoid my early mistakes.

Leadership fundamentals

◼ **Tell colleagues where they are heading:**

Identify the vision – decide what you want to achieve.

Example: We need to show more obvious use of maths across the curriculum.

Create the strategies – work out how you are going to get there.

Example: Identify a school where they have addressed this successfully and analyse their processes.

Get colleagues onside:

Make sure you invite them to join the team.

Example: Include everyone who has any level of input into this project.

Tell people what your vision is and seek their support.

Example: Get the evidence (for example, national statistics/examples of good practice). Make it clear to everyone involved.

Encourage everyone to believe in what you are going to do:

Example: Lay out the reasons for doing this work. Highlight the benefits. Note the dangers of not doing it.

Give colleagues a clear sense of direction.

Example: Let them know how the work is going. Communicate successes and failures.

Motivate your team:

Make colleagues feel that they are part of the change taking place and that it's not being "done to them".

Example: Recognise every success to ensure that your team feel it is worthwhile.

Spread the word outside of your team. Let the whole school know how things are going. (There is more about motivation in Chapter 4.)

Management fundamentals

Check the budget:

Early in the planning stage, you need to find out if your proposals are affordable. You might have an allocated budget to work from or you could be expected to ask permission from the school business manager. This is very important. It is pointless pushing ahead with a change project only to find that it can't be funded.

Plan the project:

Meticulously set out the steps that you're going to take.

Make sure each step has the funding it needs.

Decide who is going to be responsible for the different aspects of the project. Tell your colleagues exactly what is expected of them.

Set up monitoring and evaluation points:

Have a clear and realistic timetable of checkpoints. Be open about what you will be looking for and when this will be taking place.

Tell your colleagues all the details. Make sure they understand your expectations.

In my years of being led, the single most-common failing has been a lack of communication from senior colleagues. This has caused no end of confusion and distrust. Do your best to keep your team informed and maintain open communication with those above you.

What do you think – leadership or management?

Have a go at categorising the steps in this scenario. You'll soon see which is which.

Scenario: You are head of maths in the school. An inspection has noted that you need to have more evidence of maths being used across the curriculum. You know that work needs to be done.

Action/event	Leadership, management or both?
You arrange a meeting and discuss your vision with the principal.	Arranging the meeting: *management*. Discussing your vision: *leadership*.
The principal agrees and allocates you a 20-minute time slot at next month's whole-school staff meeting.	
You present your case at the meeting in an organised and professional style.	
At the meeting, the principal fully supports you.	

Action/event	Leadership, management or both?
The principal arranges cover for you so that you can visit "St Wonderful" school.	
You visit and make copious notes to support your proposed action.	
You arrange an after-school meeting with the principal to discuss your findings.	
The principal is impressed and gives you a £1,500 budget to develop your initiative.	
You notice a two-day training course "Mathematics Across the Curriculum: Be Inspection Compliant" that fits your needs perfectly and decide to attend.	
You get the go-ahead from the principal and book the course. The course fee, two days of supply cover, overnight stay and travel fall within budget.	
The principal tells you to run a workshop during the next INSET day.	
You plan the workshop content.	
You organise rooms, resources and groups.	
You provide pre-training information for colleagues.	
You deliver the training and distribute evaluation forms.	

Leadership types and styles

Most leadership training courses spend time looking at different types of leader and leadership styles. This is valuable, but I didn't think it appropriate to go into too much detail here. There is plenty of information online, so have a search if you are interested or want to take your leadership studies further.

I compiled a list of styles that I have come across in my research and experience: autocratic, democratic, strategic, transformational, transactional, team-led, cross-cultural, facilitative, laissez-faire, coaching, charismatic, visionary, instructional, surgeon, soldier, accountant, philosopher, architect, situational, servant, adaptive, affiliative, democratic, pacesetting and commanding. I stopped at 25, so there will be some that I've missed out.

In *The Positive Leader*, Jan Mühlfeit and Melina Costi (2017) reckon that there are up to 850 definitions of leadership. They suggest that you google these rather than expect them to list them all. I'm following their approach. That said, it is worth noting that interest has grown around two types of leadership in the school context – *instructional* leadership and *transformational* leadership. There is debate about which is "best", which John Hattie (2012) brings into focus. Comparing them is difficult due to the differing definitions that can be applied, which may or may not fit your way of thinking.

In my opinion, one of the most straightforward definitions of transformational leadership is by Alex Schneider and Neil Burton (2008: 22), who define it as when leaders create "a high level of commitment" that comes from "strong emotional relationships between the leaders and the led". It is also described by Viviane Robinson et al. (2011: 131–132) thus:

> *Transformational leadership refers to that type of leadership which elicits unusually high levels of commitment, loyalty and energy from followers, particularly under conditions of radical or transformational change.*

In other words, people follow your lead because they want to, not because they *have* to. I think these are very useful definitions. They are concise and easy to apply.

Instructional leadership is nothing new. It seems to have its roots in research conducted in the 1980s, but it is looked upon favourably now, partly as the result of John Hattie's recent focus on visible learning. There are plenty of interesting videos on the Visible Learning website, which I'd recommend.[1] In this type of leadership, the leader is focused

---

1 See https://visible-learning.org/category/videos/.

on the curriculum and *how* it is taught. An instructional leader will be active in finding out how teachers are performing and looking at the effect they are having. Things like learning walks, lesson observations, book scrutinies and test/exam data analysis play a significant part in this leadership approach. This is a familiar strategy in UK and North American schools.

Steven Weber (2017) proposes five reasons why schools need instructional leaders:

1. To provide clarity.
2. To provide opportunities to develop and empower future leaders.
3. To provide the opportunity for continuous improvement.
4. To provide the opportunity to establish goals.
5. To provide the opportunity for improved alignment.

My understanding of transformational leadership leads me to think that instructional leadership can be part of a transformational approach, not at odds with it.

As a middle leader, if you have sourced the evidence you need in order to make changes, then you should find that colleagues understand why changes need to be made. They buy into your ideas because they can see why you had them. Without getting into an academic debate, I suggest that a highly effective leader will be using the tools of instructional leadership in order to produce the evidence needed to convince colleagues to support them.

One final leadership style to think about here is *situational* leadership. This is where a leader adapts their style to the needs of colleagues and the school as the current situation demands. It is an adaptive approach which suggests that good leaders don't get stuck in one way of working. I cannot imagine a popular and effective leader who doesn't work in this way.

Honest reflection

Think of the leaders in your current school (or previous schools). You don't need to name them, just list the skills they had or lacked. What was the result?

Make a note of:

- What made things work.
- What had a negative effect.

For example:

Leader	Leadership skills	Management skills	Which meant that:
Leader A	Very good at telling people what their vision was. *Not very good at getting everyone on board.*	Good with the budget. *Sometimes didn't monitor what was happening.*	We all knew what we were aiming for. There was never a time when we ran out of funding to keep things going. *Leader A often didn't realise that some of the team weren't getting involved. This slowed things down and led to a couple of unhappy team members.*

Use this experience to help steer you away from the things that didn't work and towards the things that did.

Concluding thoughts

Be aware of the skills you need to be applying in any given situation and don't forget to tell your team what you are doing.

Watch what good senior leaders are doing as well as learning from experienced middle leaders.

Don't forget, there is a lot to read out there.

Chapter 2
Leadership Dispositions:
How Successful Leaders Behave

There are three essentials to leadership: humility, clarity and courage.

Attributed to Fuchan Yuan

By the end of this chapter, you will be more aware of the dispositions you need to be a successful and respected leader. This will help you build a strong profile and get things done. This could be the most important part of the book, because everything else you do as a leader will be influenced by what you think about here.

There are a lot of references to leadership dispositions in official documents produced by those responsible for education across the globe. The Australian Institute of Teaching and School Leadership's (2017: 21) professional standards for school leaders refer to principals behaving "with integrity underpinned by moral purpose". Empathy, resilience and personal well-being are recognised, and leaders are expected "to build trust across the school community and to create a positive learning atmosphere for students and staff" (Australian Institute of Teaching and School Leadership, 2017: 23). In the United States, the *North Carolina Standards for School Executives* (2013) talks about, amongst other things, using data effectively. But underpinning this is the desire that this is done with "open, honest communication" and leadership that is "ethical and principled" (Public Schools of North Carolina, 2013: 2). In Yukon, Canada, the *Educational Leadership Framework for Yukon Principals and Vice-Principals* (2011: 5) highlights the "individual ethical values and beliefs that guide their moral compass as educational leaders".

In England, the *National Standards of Excellence for Headteachers* (2015) outlines a number of "qualities and knowledge" benchmarks under the label "Domain One", which, it can be argued, is a set of dispositions. The General Teaching Council for Scotland has an Interpersonal Skills and Abilities section in its 2012 *Standards for Leadership and Management*.

Before going any further, it is a good idea to establish what dispositions are. For the purpose of this chapter, let's go with my definition:

Dispositions: qualities of mind and character that influence behaviours.

There is a lot of advice and guidance about *what* you have to do as a leader, but it is *how* you go about these things that makes the difference between, for example, success and failure, or being respected and being despised.

Think about teaching a very good lesson: it is not just about what you want the class to learn but how you deliver it that will make the difference. It is not enough to have deep knowledge of your subject if you have no idea how to communicate it. Let's face it, ticking off content is easy. In the same way, ticking off a to-do list of leadership and management tasks is not difficult. As learning professionals, we are used to thinking hard about lesson delivery, but we tend not to give so much time to thinking about how we apply our leadership practices.

Honest reflection

Where are you now?

How often do you think about the type of leadership behaviour you are exhibiting at work?

Never	Seldom	Sometimes	Regularly	Very often
It's never crossed my mind. *I go about my daily work without giving it any consideration.*	Hardly ever. *If I do, I don't reflect on what I've done.*	Now and again I wonder how well I've dealt with something. *I might think about doing things differently, but I usually carry on as before.*	I often think about the way I've reacted to something. *I'll reflect on it and modify my behaviour next time if needed.*	I constantly reflect on my actions. *These thoughts genuinely shape my next steps. I see this as part of my professional development.*

Please don't regard the ideas later in this chapter as a list of characteristics and traits to be put into a checklist and ticked off. A lot of the time they will be personal to you and will depend on the context of your workplace. Understanding how dispositions affect what you do on a daily basis is part of being a successful leader.

Why are dispositions important?

You will have noticed that leaders can be unpopular at times.

Honest reflection

Recall when you have disliked or lost respect for a leader (or when colleagues have voiced their displeasure).

What were the reasons for this reaction? Make a note of them.

By doing this, you will have a model of what *not* to do and what to avoid.

You could take a risk and ask colleagues the question: "What has made you disrespect a leader?"

Our profession is under a huge amount of pressure from different directions and those in leadership positions can get caught in the crossfire. This is especially so for middle leaders who have to follow instructions from above and react to the responses from led colleagues. It gets particularly difficult when you might not totally agree with a senior management message that you have to deliver. Rest assured that almost every middle leader in any organisation across the world will have been in this situation. It is a fundamental part of the role. There are some suggestions about how to deal with this in Chapter 7.

There are some parts of the job that are easy and rewarding – praising and congratulating colleagues, for example. But having to criticise and even impose some sort of sanction is tough. You will have to make some difficult decisions, and using your dispositions appropriately will make this easier. How you go about these aspects of your job is very important. It can be the difference between receiving a hearty acceptance, a grudging acceptance or a volatile verbal outburst. Or perhaps something worse, such as a complaint being lodged against you.

What do dispositions look like in our work?

Here is a good one to start with:

Civility – showing politeness and respect to others

Consider this for a moment.

Honest reflection

Can you think of an instance when a senior colleague has been rude to you or someone you work with? Perhaps a friend who works in another school has told you about an experience they've had.

Or how about a time when someone above you in the hierarchy has been curt, off-hand or dismissive?

If you've been in the same job for some time, has this got worse over the years?

Take a couple of minutes to write down some thoughts.

Manners are worth considering. Christine Porath and Christine Pearson (2013) report that rudeness at work is on the increase and a lot of us who work in schools can recognise this well. Incivility causes damage that might not be obvious to the instigator. Porath and Pearson's research, reported in the *Harvard Business Review*, in this area is substantial, with findings from 800 leaders across 17 industries. They note that where workers have been on the receiving end of incivility:

- *48% intentionally decreased their work effort.*
- *47% intentionally decreased the time spent at work.*
- *38% intentionally decreased the quality of their work.*
- *78% said their commitment to the organization declined.*
- *12% said that they left their job because of the uncivil treatment.*
- *25% admitted to taking their frustration out on customers.*

Never	Seldom	Sometimes	Regularly	Very often
It's not something I've ever con-sidered.	*If I'm really stuck on some-thing, I might ask.*	*It is part of my practice, but only now and then.*	*I consult on most things and this is rec-ognised by my led colleagues.*	*I will go to my led colleagues on virtually every occasion. They expect to be consulted on all issues relating to their work.*

Example 3: Giving credit and thanks.

> *"… be quick to pass on the credit where it's due."* (Veland, 2012: 46)

This respondent points out that any credit or recognition that your school gets from an outside source should be shared by everyone. It's not just about you; it's your team's success.

Honest reflection

Draw three columns on a piece of paper: one headed "recognised", one "not recognised" and the other "my feelings".

Write down any examples of successes that you and your colleagues have had and whether or not they were recognised by senior colleagues. Use the third column to record how you felt about it then and/or now.

If you are already in a middle leadership position, repeat this exercise but think about:

▪ Times when you've recognised your colleagues' work, or not. How do you think they felt?

▪ Filling it in from a led colleague's perspective.

There is more discussion of recognition in Chapter 4.

Honesty – being truthful and straightforward

Example 1: Addressing problems with an open mind without personal prejudice. This can happen when things aren't going well and a led colleague needs to be spoken to. Try not to take sides or let previous incidents cloud your judgement. We'll cover more on this later.

Example 2: Giving clear, waffle-free answers will help colleagues know where they stand. Being kept in the dark about the reasons behind decisions can eat away at people. For example, the SLT trying to convince everyone that there isn't a behaviour problem in the school when there clearly is will only do damage in the long run.

Great leaders are almost always great simplifiers, who can cut through argument, debate, and doubt to offer a solution everybody can understand.

Attributed to Colin Powell

Empathy – being able to understand and share the feelings of others

This doesn't always have to mean saying "I've been in your shoes", trying to take on other peoples' emotions or attempting to please everyone. How often can we say that we've been in *exactly* the same situation as someone else? Empathy is about the thoughtful consideration of others' feelings (Goleman, 2004).

Example 1: I know of two local schools that had poor inspection outcomes four years ago. One head teacher told the whole staff that this would mean possible job losses due to the probable falling roll and said to expect more lesson observations and book scrutiny. The principal of the other school went around and met heads of department and teachers in their classrooms, where she explained her disbelief. She asked how they could go about improving things together. The second school is now good. The first struggles to keep any decent staff and the outcomes are far from great. The difference can be attributed, to some degree at least, to empathy from the leadership.

Being empathetic can also bring its own problems, however:

Example 2: Knowing what it's like to be overwhelmed by work and shielding colleagues from it.

"As far as a weakness goes … I don't delegate enough. I guess that empathy always holds me back … I almost don't want to put more on another individual because we are all so busy already." (Veland, 2012: 44)

Case study

"One evening I got back to my office quite late. There was a light coming from my line manager's office. Curious, I knocked and was invited in. There was my line manager, surrounded by piles of assignments that she was marking. This was surprising as I thought that all the marking for the term had been done. It turned out that these were all the late submissions from across the programme that she led. She was doing all the marking herself because she didn't want to give the rest of us any more work to do. As commendable as that was, she couldn't sustain this level of work. 'Too much' empathy can be a curse."

Chris, senior lecturer

Example 3: Not appreciating the immediacy of a problem that new colleagues are facing.

An example is behaviour management. When a new colleague is experiencing a challenging class, it is easy to say, "I remember what that was like when I was starting out. It'll get better. Believe me." This might be reassuring for some led colleagues, but you are not helping to solve the immediate problem. *It'll be better in two years* won't help when you've got that awkward class in five minutes' time.

Think how it was for you in the early days and do something to help them. Here is an example from an old colleague of mine:

Case study

"Penny had been teaching for two months. Her mentor remarked on how 'volatile' the class had been during her recent observed lesson. The mentor immediately arranged for Penny to watch some more experienced colleagues working with the same class but didn't leave it there."

Angie, head of year

Case study

"Angie suggested some strategies that had worked for other teachers, including herself. She didn't leave me to sort it out myself or try to tell me that 'it'll work out OK'. I was really pleased about that."

Penny, newly qualified teacher (NQT)

Fairness – treating people equally by being free from prejudice

Example: Making judgements that don't favour a particular group or individual.

Nothing destroys team morale quicker than a leader giving their friend preferential treatment.

There is a very serious note here. What if you have to be critical of a friend who is now a led colleague? This can be a challenge that comes with internal promotion.

Honest reflection

Have you experienced unfairness? It is important to recognise why you think that a senior colleague's actions were not fair, so write down your thoughts.

Now consider how you would have acted if the roles were reversed. How would you ensure that your actions were not seen as unfair?

Next, find a colleague and discuss your view. What do they think?

Case study

"I arrived as the new guy in January. The assistant head who was in charge of time-tabling gave me my work allocation for the rest of the year. After the first round of the two-week timetable, I realised that I had been allocated the toughest Year 9 groups. I was tipped off by a sympathetic colleague who told me that the assistant head's cricket club mate got the easiest groups. It still sticks in my memory. And it was a long time ago!"

Bill, secondary history and PE teacher

Being fair moves us on to the next disposition. Perhaps there are some overlaps.

Integrity – being able to stick to the ethical code

Doing what is right and having strong moral principles seems an obvious requirement, but there are leaders who don't demonstrate this disposition. Bronagh Munro (2019) reports on organised cheating in UK academies, whilst Richard Fausset and Alan Blinder (2015) report in *The New York Times* that educators in Atlanta have even been sent to prison for cheating. Narrowing the curriculum, anyone?

Consider this quote:

"I found out some very disturbing information and had to turn that information over to the proper authorities even though it was a very prominent member of our

community." He added further, "I really had no choice, first of all, ethically, and second of all because it was the right thing to do." (Veland, 2012: 55)

Although we don't know the details of this situation, it sounds serious. I suggest that "doing the right thing" is far easier if the behaviour is clearly wrong – for example, an inadequate response to safeguarding issues. But what if the incident is not as serious, but still wrong? Is there ever a time when a leader can justifiably think it best to turn a blind eye?

Honest reflection

Work with another colleague or, even better, two others.

Brainstorm a list of things that you (or your peers) have got away with but that you think weren't very important.

Imagine that you have discovered that one of your led colleagues has done one of the things on your list. Discuss what you would do about it. Be honest.

Is there anything you'd choose to ignore? Why would you ignore it?

What are the possible outcomes of:

▪ doing nothing?
▪ taking action?

Try to pick some borderline issues.

Does this example have any influence on how you might handle a tricky situation?

"I felt the need for everything to be done properly but at the same time, I was going to have compassion for the individuals who were affected by what this person had done and compassion for the person who did it." She correctly pointed out, "as a leader, your compassion can not be conditional." (Veland, 2012: 57)

In Todd Veland's work, and in the official standards documents from the different countries mentioned earlier, an "ethical approach" is frequently referred to. It comes down to making difficult decisions that people won't like, but that are "the right thing to do for the kids".

This deserves attention.

Current experience reflection activities

First of all, think back to a time when you have had to go with a decision made by a senior colleague. You didn't like it, but it was good for the students.

- What was the decision?
- Why didn't you like it?
- How did you react?
- From a student perspective, what would have happened if this unpopular decision hadn't been made?
- From a staff perspective, what would have happened if this unpopular decision hadn't been made?

Now think about when *you* have had to make an unpopular decision.

- What was the difficult decision?
- How did colleagues react?
- How did you address their objections?
- What would have happened if you hadn't made this unpopular decision?
- Would you do the same again, or not? Note any changes you would make.

If you haven't had to do this yet, try to imagine a situation in which you might have to in the future.

- What is the potentially unpopular decision?
- How might some colleagues react?
- How do you plan to address their objections?
- What might happen if you avoid this unpopular decision?

I hope you've managed to spend some time working through these activities. Take your thoughts with you through the rest of the book.

To end this chapter, consider the following ideas, adapted from master executive coach Susan C. Foster's article "7 Things Great Leaders Never Say". You will be able to spot the leadership and management clichés that contradict what we've looked at so far.

Four things great leaders never say

1. **"There are no problems, only solutions."**

   If you say this during a meeting, it makes you look disinterested or like you've missed the point that something is wrong. Led colleagues will feel that they are being ignored or that it's not your job to help sort things out. It will, without doubt, make you look out of touch.

   Instead: Listen and make notes. Send a message to them later in the day to thank them for their comments and concerns.

2. **"Don't do anything without asking me first."**

   Micromanagement is one of the most despised things in any organisation but especially in an environment in which creative and highly professional people work. Schools fit that description. Obviously, there will be times when you want to check that everything is going as planned, particularly if the person with the responsibility is new to the role. In fact, they will most likely be keen to have support close by, initially at least. As we will see, led colleagues will be more motivated and productive when they have been given the autonomy to get on with things.

   Instead: Be very clear about what you expect and build in time for feedback meetings.

3. **"It's not personal, it's about school."**

   This is a particularly ill-judged comment in an institution that is all about personal relationships. Work, personal performance and well-being are interlinked throughout our working day.

   Instead: Make sure that your team know that you are very concerned about them as individual human beings in a challenging workplace. Yes, difficult decisions will have to be made, but having empathy towards your led colleagues is very important.

   "My strength is people. My strength is working with them. I am passionate about making connections with people. I love the people who work for me and I hope they feel the same." (Veland, 2012: 42)

4.   **"Failure is not an option."**

This will instil fear into your team. Nobody willingly chooses failure. Such a statement will stifle any chance of creative solutions and could well lead to your colleagues becoming reluctant to suggest anything. It will be left to you as a leader to make all of the decisions and take all of the criticism: not a good situation. Don't scare your team into inaction.

Instead: Make sure that your team understands that they can try new ideas in order to move the situation forward. If mistakes are made, the team will act quickly to rectify them. This is an opportunity for you to lead by example. Make it clear that you are trying something different.

Less than a generation ago, a school leader's remit would, generally speaking, have been contained within the school in which they worked. It was unusual for a senior or middle leader to have a field of influence that went very far beyond their school walls. This is changing. For example, the introduction and expansion of multi-academy trusts (MATs), along with less formal federations and school alliances, has seen a growth in *system* leadership. This sees individuals and teams advising and training colleagues across different schools, which requires an evolving set of dispositions.

It might be helpful to refer back to this chapter as you work through Chapter 6, where we look at system leadership in more depth.

Concluding thoughts

Todd Veland (2012: 17) believes that identifying leadership dispositions should be the starting point for any organisation. I think that leader behaviour needs reviewing because school leadership is evolving. We need to use a 21st century approach.

Honest reflection

With this knowledge, how are you going to change your own practice?

What might you:

- stop doing?
- start doing?
- continue doing?

What might you ask others to:

- stop doing?
- start doing?
- continue doing?

Chapter 3

Building Your Professional Image: Looking Like a Leader

You never get a second chance to make a first impression.

Attributed to Oscar Wilde

By the end of this chapter, you should have a clear idea about how to approach your first leadership post and how to maintain that image into your career.

In middle leadership, you're not alone

Taking on any new role is challenging, but a positive thing about being a middle leader is that you won't be the only one. Here are some tips:

- Make the most of this situation by using other middle leaders' experience and expertise. Never be afraid to ask for help.
- If you aren't given a mentor, ask for one. Keep them fully up to date with your work and with how things are going.
- Try to meet middle leaders from other schools. Look out for subject or phase meetings that your group of schools/MAT/alliance are having.
- Arrange to meet up with colleagues who are in a similar situation.
- If you lead a subject area, join your subject association.

Getting together with other middle leaders is very useful. In all the training that I have done – both as a delegate and as a course leader – one thing stands out: everyone is surprised by how many other people are in the same boat. We all have similar problems and the same worries. Finding out that you are not alone is one of the best feelings. Make sure you don't miss these opportunities. The table that follows is an example of how to identify specific individuals who might be able to help you. You can compile your own list of colleagues to approach.

Identify who can help you

Current experience reflection activity				
The issue	**Who and from where?**	**Why?**	**How will you approach them?**	**When?**
Awkward established colleagues.	Jenny, Longton Academy.	She was in my position two years ago and has made good progress.	Email, then arrange to go to her school to discuss things.	Email today. Try to meet before the next staff meeting.

Being new – a chance for reinvention

Although there are strategies here that you will use more in your earlier days of leadership, there are some that you'll benefit from at every level. Some might need refining, but the underlying message will be the same. Cassandra Frangos (2018), writing in the *Harvard Business Review*, suggests that "The capacity for reinvention is the single-most-important career attribute for executives today." And reinventing yourself is exactly what you are doing when you take on a new leadership position. Start by having a clear vision of yourself as a leader and of the image you want to portray.

What sort of leader do you want to be seen as?

Sometimes it is easier to approach this type of question from a different direction. It's often easier to think about what you don't want to be. I met some leadership colleagues to think about how we would *not* want to be perceived. This is what we came up with.

We wouldn't want to be regarded as a leader who:

- Doesn't seem to be around the school much.
- Doesn't tell you how things are going.
- Isn't interested in team members.

- Doesn't lead by example.

- Is afraid to challenge decisions from above that might threaten the team.

- Is unclear about the direction in which the team is going.

- Doesn't take care with new appointments and shows bias.

- Doesn't delegate well.

- Isn't 100% sure of their role.

- Hasn't got as much expertise as everyone else.

To establish a good leadership image, don't do the things on this list. Have you had any leaders who do behave like this? It will be a good exercise for you to recall any similar instances and reflect on the impact of their behaviour in the two activities that follow.

Consider the following questions. Don't just answer "yes" or "no", but write down details to justify your response. The reason is important because it will help you link ideas together to establish the context. For example, you could say "yes" to "not being around much" but add the detail that they were new in post and had to go to training sessions. This gives a sound reason. If you add: "In their absence, they delegated their tasks well," you are identifying elements of good practice. Alternatively, if you comment: "They weren't around much. No one knew where they were," this looks like a different scenario. Use this exercise to gather your surface responses in order to delve more deeply in the honest reflection activity that follows.

Have you had a leader who:

- Wasn't around much?

- Didn't keep you informed of progress?

- Didn't delegate well?

- Didn't seem interested in you as a member of the team?

- Didn't appear to know what they were doing?

Honest reflection

Now make a note of your feelings about those individuals. Think about the effect their behaviour had on you and on your performance.

I had a leader who _____.

The reason was (and add detail) _____.

This led to me feeling _____.

As a team we _____.

Repeat this for as many examples as you can.

How will this influence your leadership practice?

Create a bullet list detailing what you will do and what you won't do.

Getting it right from the start

The image you portray from the outset is important. You need to show your authority as a leader in the same way as you do with a new class. The use of "authority" is different, however. Here the focus is on your "authoritative" persona; it is not about being authoritarian.

This is an aspect of leadership that can be particularly difficult for young leaders to navigate. In research by Karen Edge et al. (2017) into generation X leaders, it was recognised that even *how you look* can cast a negative impression. Some may think that you look too young to be a good leader. This is translated into a distrust of your ability, knowledge and understanding. It is just as bad as assuming that a leader who is older must be out of touch with new developments.

As wrong as this seems, it is the reality in a lot of schools and other workplaces. If you are a young leader, or even just look younger than your years, then you'll have to work hard on your image. Some older, more experienced colleagues might expect you to earn their respect.

Case study

"My main concerns when taking on this position were the balance of workload – I teach Year 4 – and professional jealousy, mainly because of my route into teaching and the fact I'd only been qualified for two years. Despite this, I really enjoy the role and I've embraced it. I've learned a lot and developed in confidence."

Anna, lower Key Stage 2 phase lead

Power and influence

As a leader, you find yourself with a level of power, influence and responsibility. For a lot of us starting out, having power is a new experience. We will each manage and cope with it differently. Basically, there are two types of power that inform how a leader works: formal and informal.

Formal power is given through a title – such as head teacher, head of department, phase leader and so on. These titles give leaders the authority to make decisions, give out rewards and make judgements. This is also referred to as "positional leadership": people follow you because they have to, not because they want to. John Maxwell (2013) discusses this in his talk about the five levels of leadership, a video of which is available on YouTube. He shows that positional leadership is only the first level and, as such, we need to move up and away from it as quickly as possible. Leaders whose main focus is on their position tend to be more authoritarian, and this can contribute to micromanagement.

I am sure that formal power on its own is not enough to make a truly effective leader, so it is important that you bring more to your leadership than just a positional title. It is your actions that will make this happen, which takes us back to Chapter 2.

Informal power, alongside formal power, is what you need in order to become a successful and accepted leader. As you will see, there are several types of informal power. In general, we like our leaders to be experts in their area. We expect them to have experience and an honest understanding of the work we do. Your led colleagues will rightly expect this of you from day one: so show them. This display of expertise is often referred to as "expert power". Think of it as affording you a level of credibility. Being a credible leader will allow you a lot of influence. This happens at every level.

> **Case study**
>
> "I was a nervous new head teacher. I was worried about the seniority that I had taken on, especially as my predecessor had been there for 11 years. Although I felt a bit of an imposter, my local authority link adviser helped to put my mind at rest by assuring me that my new colleagues appreciated that I had been in the classroom for getting on for 20 years. I had a high level of credibility as a teacher and that really helped."
>
> **Paul, primary head teacher**

Informal power can also come from reputation. If you have shown that you can lead well, this will have as much influence as a formal title. Respectful behaviour towards your team will increase your power. An empathetic approach, alongside a reputation for "doing the right thing", will add to it as well. As you'll see in Chapter 4, recognising team members' efforts will only enhance your informal power.

Using your knowledge and experience

The saying "knowledge is power" is true to a certain extent. But it's what you do with that knowledge that counts.

> **Case study**
>
> "When I was a new deputy head, I remember being very impressed with the head teacher's knowledge in governor meetings. The language he used, the ease with which he moved from subject to subject. No questions were left unanswered. He was in complete control. His behaviour was authoritative, not authoritarian. I thought there wasn't a chance I'd ever be in that position. But I was wrong. I signed up for a leadership training course and joined a leadership union. Then I found that I was in a position where I had to read and engage with the jargon and the current school leadership issues. Before long I was in that authoritative position."
>
> **Simon, secondary deputy head**

In the same way as Simon, you will probably have access to information that not every-one else has. This can be an eye-opener when you are new in post. This is a new level of responsibility and it is how you deal with it that counts. Think about the dispositions of integrity and honesty that we've talked about. The formal power is in having access to the information. The informal power is in how you use the information, and that is the key. Be seen as indiscreet and any respect you have attracted will soon disappear. It won't matter how much formal power you have, you will face an uphill battle from then on.

If you show that you are an honest person and an expert in your field, you are likely to be naturally powerful. This, in turn, will give you confidence, which will make you feel more at ease. A confident leader who knows what they are talking about and who is at ease in their job is a leader for whom we would all like to work.

Simon was surprised about how much he didn't know, but he made the right connec-tions to put that right. Identify the areas that you think you need to know more about. Then plan how to address them. Use the example below to copy and complete your own table, adding as many ideas as you can.

Current experience reflection activity		
Things I need to know more about	**How to address this**	**This will help me to**
Leadership and manage-ment jargon.	Join a leadership asso-ciation. Attend their meetings. Subscribe to their newsletters.	Understand and con-tribute to leadership meetings at a profes-sional level.

It is worth talking to other, more experienced middle leaders to find out what they have learned since taking up the post. You are entering a work environment where you won't know what you don't know, so learn from others to save time.

Who do you think could help you? Use the table as a prompt for your reflections.

Current experience reflection activity			
Who to approach	**Because**	**What to ask**	**Their response**
Charlotte.	She started as subject lead two years ago and has been very successful.	What came as a surprise to you when you started?	How difficult it is to manage a budget that has already been allocated by your predecessor.

Proving yourself in the early days

It's a good thing to listen to some advice before you start. Here are some ideas.

Make it all about your colleagues

You are there to make a difference in a new job. Your focus must be on how things are going and what needs to be done to make improvements. If you have moved to a new school, find out how things are done there. You will need to understand the culture before making any decisions. Don't forget how to treat your colleagues – humility, as a new leader, will go a long way.

Your new colleagues need to see that they are your main concern and that you care about them professionally. Have a meeting with them early on. Try to have a whole-team meeting, then follow this up with seeing everyone individually. Use the following questions to form the basis of your meetings. They are not meant to be perfectly formed, but rather a starting point for you to adapt as you need.

- What are the most important issues facing this department/age phase in the next year?
- How do you think we should go about solving this problem?
- What do you like about working here?
- What's not so good? (This can be easy to ask when you're new.)
- What are the most challenging/rewarding things about working here?
- (Add some of your own questions.)

In Chapter 5, we'll see the importance of consulting colleagues about major issues. It is a good thing for you to do as a new manager, so talk to your experienced colleagues.

Don't be an AMOS (at my old school ...)

I made this mistake. As a new deputy head, I often mentioned how we did things at my previous school. It wasn't until a colleague suggested that if it was so good, I ought to go back there that I realised what a bore I was being. Obviously, you will be expected to bring experience to your role. Perhaps you were given the job because of success in a specific field – raising standards in a particular area is a common example. If this is the case, then colleagues will want to know how you managed it, but this is more about *your* performance rather than how wonderful your previous school is. No one wants a new leader to try to force them to become a version of the last place in which they worked.

Case study

"In one school, we had been very successful for years. It was a very happy place to work. OK, it was a bit 'traditional' in some parts, but we all knew this and it worked for us. Then this new head arrived. It was barely two weeks before he told us that we were all pretty useless. Then he told us to throw out a lot of the resources we had. He replaced them with stuff we knew nothing about. We had no real idea of what we were doing. The standards we had maintained before dropped. It was weird. The parents didn't get it either. They got really agitated. The place started to fall apart. Some of the people I worked with, who were also my mates, left. It all ended with a nasty taste. What made it worse was his constant going on about how they did things in his last school. I got out 18 months later. He left a term after that."

Liz, primary deputy head

Can you think of any initiatives that new leaders have introduced? Reflect on the effects.

Current experience reflection activity		
What was it?	**How soon in post?**	**What was the effect?**
New principal: scrapped having to hand in plans for the week.	Immediately.	Everyone appreciated the trust and lighter workload.
New head of department: introduced unannounced learning walks.	Half a term.	An atmosphere of fear developed. Some colleagues became real creeps.

Invite feedback

The single best thing a new executive can do to avoid a brief tenure is to actively pursue feedback. Most undergo rigorous executive assessments prior to receiving an offer, but soon they are too occupied with the demands of the job to be introspective. (Frangos, 2018)

Joseph Folkman (2015) has collected clear evidence which suggests that leaders who ask for feedback from colleagues are the most effective. He says his data "shows an exceptionally strong correlation between asking for feedback and overall effectiveness of leaders". He also found that top-ranked leaders are better at asking for feedback.

It might be difficult to ask for feedback early in role, but don't let that stop you. At your first team meeting, ask your colleagues what they expect from you. I suggest that you tell your team that you will be doing this in an introductory email, sent to them before the start of term. This preparation sends out a positive message and will also help avoid awkward silences when you meet. Once you have an idea of their expectations, you can then track your progress throughout the year.

Here's an example. Ask your colleagues to record their expectations. Encourage them to revisit the list at regular intervals and write down their thoughts about the progress being made. Use the following table as an example to structure your records.

Current experience reflection activity			
Expectation	**Half-term feedback**	**[Other checkpoints feedback]**	**End-of-year feedback**
Clear communication of new initiative's progress.	New marking scheme explained well. Input from us encouraged. Objectives very clear.	TAs monthly meeting. Initially they felt included, but now they feel increasingly ignored.	Went well initially but communication dwindled as the year went by. Easter saw a big drop in meetings and messages. Not clear if we were meeting the objectives set out in September.

You will need to add more checkpoints, but this type of feedback from colleagues will help you a lot. It's not just feedback on your performance that is useful in building a good reputation in leadership, it's critical to have a good understanding of *why* colleagues hold those beliefs. This will help you adjust your leadership strategies and behaviours in the future.

This is a good example of professional development through experience. Asking for feedback will help you to become known as a leader who wants to improve. You are unlikely to be regarded as someone who relies solely on the authority of a title.

Honest reflection

If you have had the chance to feed back to a senior colleague, reflect on:

■ How easy/challenging it was to be completely honest.

■ The effect it had on the leader's practice.

■ How much you valued the process.

■ Your professional feeling towards the leader in question. (For example, did they seem more trustworthy or approachable?)

- Whether the feedback you offered is something you would be happy to follow yourself.
- Whether soliciting feedback from your led colleagues is something you would be happy to do.

Your thoughts here will determine how you approach asking for feedback and your subsequent actions.

Be confident – try not to be negative

There are times when we might think that anyone could do our job. This is not the case. Be confident in the fact that if a led colleague is critical of your performance, they probably couldn't do it as well as you, and they know it. Life is full of individuals who like to pull apart those in positions that they themselves have never experienced. Once you know that, things become easier.

Self-doubt is a common state of mind in new middle leaders. Don't let that worry you. It happens all the time. I worked with a head teacher who would only stay at a school for a maximum of three years. "After that, they find you out!" was her favourite advice. She appeared calm, confident and completely in control, but it was all a façade. She could well have been suffering from imposter syndrome, something that is increasingly recognised as a genuine psychological state. Andy Molinsky (2016), a professor of organisational behaviour, tells us that even the then CEO and president of Starbucks, Howard Schultz, felt the same way when heading up the giant corporation. In an article called "Everyone Suffers from Imposter Syndrome – Here's How to Handle It", he suggests that recognising the *benefits* of being new is a good strategy. This is constructive advice and will help you approach challenges with a positive and confident outlook. An example is if you come across problems that have deep roots in the past. You will be able to tell people that you have absolutely no bias based on preconceived opinions. This is a strong place to be; however, it could still be a problem area for new leaders because some colleagues might use your newness as an opportunity to unload grievances from the past.

Honest reflection

As a new leader, how would you react to someone telling you about an issue that had caused problems in the past, for which they were blaming others?

Give this careful consideration. Write down what your strategy, as a new leader, would be.

Points to consider:

- Being fair.
- Being open-minded.

See Chapter 7 for more strategies, especially the fact-finding suggestions on pages 113–114.

Consider this issue pre-emptively to avoid being caught out later.

Another way of combatting self-doubt is to never lose sight of the fact that you have been promoted on merit. Senior leaders do not usually take a gamble when making appointments. To make sure you never lose sight of this, copy and complete the following table. Go through your job application and look for the strengths you listed: add these to the left-hand column. This way you will give yourself evidence that you are living up to expectations. You are proving that you can do what you claim.

Current experience reflection activity		
Strength	**Which means I can**	**Examples**
Team player.	Bring people together. It's about *us*, not individuals.	Got the team together to talk about the run of poor lesson observations. Offered support, reassurance and guidance.
High knowledge levels.	Inform and support.	Some of the team not clear on the new phonics teaching resources. Provided one-to-one training to meet specific needs.

Revisit this list and use it as affirmation. You have proof that you can do the job. Also, it will be good to list the things which you perceive as a strength but for which you lack evidence. Put some checkpoints in with a view to gathering this evidence. This will be an excellent development tool.

Here's an example:

Strength to be evidenced	Suggested activity	Date
Classroom expertise: behaviour management strategies.	Two NQTs to watch me teach.	By October half term.

This exercise will reaffirm your confidence in your own ability (and most of us need that from time to time). You are clearly stating that you know what you need to do to improve. It is honest and constructive. There is a similar exercise on pages 53–54 that looks at the "essentials" of middle leadership.

Show appreciation

Letting new colleagues know how pleased you are to be working with them will go a long way. Show appreciation of the work they have done. If you think that some things haven't been very good, then recognise the challenges they have faced. For example, if they have had a bad inspection report, don't dwell on the negatives but illustrate how they have the skills to turn things around. Do this by identifying what they do well as individuals and as a team. Leave the difficult conversations for when you know your colleagues better. Get them on your side first by showing them that you are on theirs. It's not unknown for new leaders at any level to be overcritical of what has been done before. This is disrespectful and will make you very unpopular, which will be a barrier to any changes you want to make. A good time and place to convey this message is at your first team meeting. Prepare your introductory speech carefully because it will set the tone for your working relationships.

Make your expectations clear

Early in post, make sure that everyone knows what the team is working towards. Then keep telling them. This is a key point that we'll explore in depth in Chapter 5.

- Make your intended goals clear and identify where the checkpoints are going to be.

- Present your team with a clear timetable and cycle of events. Remove the guesswork.

This will let everybody know that you are here to do a specific job and you have a clear structure in mind. It was interesting to see research reported by Mattson Newell (2018) for Partners in Leadership. They found that 85% of employees were unclear about what they were trying to achieve. They talk about how dangerous it can be to not know where the finish line is.

Although we wouldn't expect the percentage to be this high in a school setting, confusion does happen. Lack of clarity can lead to a drop in motivation. Colleagues will not want to get involved if they don't know what's going on. Don't let the culture of your team just happen: lead it. Consider this as you read Chapter 5.

Be credible

Whilst no one appreciates it if you bore them with what you did in your previous school, it can be useful to drop comments into conversations to let them know that you have expertise. When a led colleague comes for advice on how to control an unruly class during their last lesson on a wet Thursday afternoon, you can say, "I know just what it feels like. I found that this strategy worked quite well for me …" Or, when one of your reception class colleagues complains about how hard it is to get certain characters to join in with activities, offer to come along to their next lesson to try out some ideas.

Beware!

This is a good place to introduce a word of caution. Because someone has shown their faith in you by giving you your first leadership role, you might think that you have to be the most perfect, most effective leader from day one. This can lead to you trying too hard to make changes and to be seen to make a difference. Don't do this. You do not want to appear to be a know-all or someone who is overconfident. If colleagues think that you are big-headed when you have just arrived, it will take a long time to get rid of that image.

Internal promotion – leading your peers

It is not unusual for teachers to be promoted to middle leadership in the school where they already work. Obviously, this will change the working relationships you have with your colleagues. You aren't an equal in the team anymore; you are now one of the bosses.

There are advantages and disadvantages to internal promotion.

Advantages:

- You know the systems.
- You have an insight into the strengths and weaknesses of the department.
- You know the people.
- You know the whole-school expectations.

Disadvantages:

- You can be too close to the situation to see any problems.
- You are not on an equal footing with your peers anymore. What you say and do will have more impact.
- Your professional image must not slip. You cannot be seen to be taking your responsibilities lightly.
- The way in which you comment on your former equals' work needs to be refined. There needs to be a "professional distance".
- Colleagues won't confide in you in the same way as before.
- It can be hard to treat friends in a new way. You can't be seen to favour them, yet some will expect you to.

Honest reflection

Imagine that you have had an internal promotion after five years in a school. You have made some good friends. You know that one of your team doesn't circulate around the class very well. In fact, they make it look like they are sitting with one group and helping them, but they are actually doing some marking or even some online shopping.

They have told you this and you have laughed about it with them.

As their new line manager:

- What are you going to do?
- How are you going to approach it?

Write your ideas down, then find a colleague and try them out. Perhaps try a role-play in which your colleague plays the part of the online shopper (or choose any realistic scenario). Don't forget the key leadership dispositions. You must be seen to be:

- Doing the right thing for the whole team.
- Fair to everyone involved.
- Led by facts and evidence.
- Empathetic.
- Showing compassion to all parties.

This will start to prepare you for dealing with these situations. You might not agree with all these bullet points, so think about your alternatives.

Having the "perfect strategy" to react to a problem is good, but I think the real answer lies in conflict avoidance – and, no, I don't mean running away from it.

Preparing to avoid conflict

Being aware of potential problems is useful. It is certainly an advantage of internal promotion. I suggest that right at the beginning of your new role, you set out your boundaries very clearly. It is better to do this before you actually start doing the job – perhaps just before the end of the previous term. It is easier to talk about potentially contentious issues before you are in post.

As hard as it may be, you need to get used to the idea that you won't be universally popular in the new position you hold. It can be a time of real tension for some. There are those who will say that this is why you shouldn't be good friends with your colleagues, but that's a debate for another time. Perhaps we need to be aware of the possible problems that come with an internal promotion before applying for one. Because you will know a lot about your team, a good tool to use is a SWOT (strengths, weaknesses, opportunities, threats) analysis. This will help to lay out the whole situation in front of you and identify issues that will need to be addressed.

SWOT analysis example

Strengths	Weaknesses
Age phase/department has good reputation. Well-regarded at last inspection. Strong team members (name them if you like). Low staff turnover. Team all agree on common aims.	Complacent at times. Occasionally, "passengers" let others do the work. Other phases are improving quicker.
Opportunities	**Threats**
Better budget allocation compared to others. Subject regarded as important by parents. New principal interested in developing the phase/department.	Possible financial cutbacks next year. Two of the team are looking to leave. Difficult year group arriving next year. Attitude of certain colleagues.

Maintaining your professional image

Sometimes SLTs are criticised because they appear to be losing contact with the main purpose of teaching. It's not uncommon to hear comments like: "I'm criticised about my teaching by someone who has never taught this year group" or "My behaviour management is graded as inadequate by someone who never teaches apart from select A level groups."

This is less of a problem for middle leaders because you are more likely to have a teaching timetable, so use this to your advantage as much as you can. Remind colleagues that you know exactly what it is like. If you have had a problem with a class that others struggle with, tell them. Share your ideas for sorting things out.

The snag here, though, is that your workload can get out of hand. You could well find yourself in a position in which your teaching is taking up so much of your time that your leadership duties are suffering. Let's face it, you'll want to be seen as a good teacher, and you need to lead by example. So you'll need to take the time to plan and assess as you always have, but leadership tasks will eat into it. I can hear the cynics shouting, "Yes, but you have additional time for leadership work!" The truth is that leadership time is often not enough. It is not unusual for middle leaders to find themselves in a tricky situation in which they don't have enough time to do either part of the role properly.

> ## Case study
>
> "I used to think I was a pretty good teacher, but now I reckon I'm a reasonable teacher and a leader who's just about OK."
>
> **Rachel, Year 4 teacher and humanities lead**

It is important to make sure that your line managers understand your workload. Make sure that you have a clear idea of what is expected of you. When we come to Chapter 8, you'll find some additional ideas to help you.

Development points to consider

People will judge you on how well you lead your team: indeed, your image will depend on this. It works both ways, from the colleagues who you lead to those who lead you. With this in mind, Chapter 4 contains strategies that will help you to be seen as a very effective leader by those on all levels of the hierarchy. But first, let's consider a few final points.

Beware arrogance. The know-all who belittles and patronises colleagues will gain little trust. There will be times when the "knowledge differential" – i.e. that you know more about the issue from your position as a leader – should be acknowledged, quite rightly, but not at the expense of disparaging your led colleagues. It can be constructive for leaders to admit to not knowing everything. We're back at the *humility* disposition.

It is often a challenge to identify your weaknesses but don't shy away from this. In order to build and maintain expertise it is important to know what you don't know. Read blogs, then engage with the ideas. Contribute to discussions on social media. This will add to your depth of dialogue and help you develop your vocabulary. You'll need to be *current*, so read as much as you can. Widen your engagement with research. Academic sources will yield a lot. Quoting recent research which is linked to your practice can only add to your expert image. It is never a bad thing to let others know what you know, so think about publicising (in a modest way) any training you've been on. My advice would be:

▦ Look for a seminar on the new curriculum, then when you get back, deliver it as part of a staff training event. Better still, show your practical application.

▦ Don't just feed back about the behaviour management course you attended. Be seen in the corridor putting it into practice.

▦ Always keep a keen eye on what might be needed in future. Being seen as an innovator is no bad thing. Just be careful about how you introduce new strategies. Avoid innovation saturation.

▦ Build the trust of your colleagues and do whatever you can to maintain it.

Kanter's Law

This is a critical piece of advice for leaders. Professor Rosabeth Moss Kanter's (2013) TED Talk is very illuminating. I have taken the liberty of pulling out the headline points and adapting them to our work.

A good leader is someone who is seen to:

▦ **Show up.** Being available and visible will build your image. Just being around will have a positive impact, and knowing this will help your self-confidence grow.

▦ **Speak up.** Being open and telling the school community about your team's work can shape the agenda and influence other people's thinking.

▦ **Look up.** This is about looking beyond the immediate day-to-day concerns and having a "noble purpose". An example might be recognising that school life is not only about test results.

▦ **Team up.** A leader who forms partnerships is likely to be successful because they know that no one can do the hard stuff on their own. This type of middle leader will look for help from within the team and build genuine team spirit. But it is also about looking outside of the team, such as learning from different heads of department and collaborating with leaders of different key stages.

▦ **Lift others up.** This plays a significant part in motivating colleagues and we'll consider this again in Chapter 4. This type of leader will share success and give credit in order to build trust and loyalty.

■ **Never give up.** These colleagues know that "everything can look like a failure in the middle": this final point is Kanter's Law.

You will have noticed that several points keep reappearing in this chapter. They are commonly regarded as good practice, so put them into your daily leadership routines. Use the "Stop, start, continue" exercise at the end of this chapter to plan how you might do this. Remember these points as you work through Chapter 4.

Some essentials – the things you need to do well

A sure-fire way of building and maintaining a strong professional image is to know what the essentials of your post are, then show people how effective you are in these areas. Your understanding of the essentials of middle leadership needs to be clear for all to see. It is well understood that if there is an area that you are weaker in, you should look for ways to improve. However, to emphasise your skills, make sure colleagues can see your new-found ability.

You will be given a precise idea of the essential requirements when you apply for a job. They should be written into the job specification/description. Some general points are noted in the following table, so add any that you think are appropriate. Copy and complete this grid to identify what you can do and how you are going to demonstrate this – I've provided a few examples. Importantly, look for the areas that need improving.

Current experience reflection activity			
The essential	**The evidence I have of this**	**The way I am going to show it**	**How to improve**
Have a deep understanding of the curriculum and any statutory and non-statutory guidance.	*I have written a detailed scheme of work that is fully cross-referenced to the national curriculum.*	*Present to colleagues and ask for suggestions on how to develop it.*	

The essential	The evidence I have of this	The way I am going to show it	How to improve
Be an expert on assessment procedures, both internal and external.	*Helped to administer national tests at previous school.*		*Need to build experience of setting internal assessment procedures that reflect whole-school policies.*
Be able to write clear policies.			
Have high credibility.			
Know how to put monitoring and evaluating systems in place.			
Have sharp knowledge of the strengths and weaknesses of the team.			
Show that your leadership work is reflecting whole-school aims.			
Be a change agent.			

To finish this chapter, it is worth considering the four Ps that, according to Timothy J. McClimon (2018), are exhibited by successful leaders:

1. **Purpose:** The need for a clear reason for doing something. A good idea of where they are going.

2. **Plan:** A precise idea of how they are going to get there.

3. **People:** Colleagues who are committed to the purpose and the plan.

4. **Power:** Support given from higher up the chain.

Be seen as someone who has these components and your image will be strong.

Concluding thoughts

It's not just how you set yourself up to make an impact when you start a leadership role, but how you work to maintain that professional image.

Honest reflection

With this knowledge, to what extent are you likely to change your practice?

What might you:

- stop doing?
- start doing?
- continue doing?

With this knowledge, to what extent are you likely to encourage others to change their practice?

What might you ask others to:

- stop doing?
- start doing?
- continue doing?

To hold yourself accountable, put some timings and deadlines in where possible.

Chapter 4

Leading Your Team: The Essence of Middle Leadership

A leader takes people where they want to go. A great leader takes people where they don't necessarily want to go, but ought to be.

Rosalynn Carter, quoted in Kara Goldin (2018)

By the end of this chapter, you will have an understanding of how to build and lead a team by motivating its members.

Positive teams work best

The hardest teams to lead are the ones in which there is a lot of negativity. It could be several people causing this or just one or two. The reasons behind this can come from several sources, but generally attitude problems are worsened by fast-paced, unsupported and imposed change, as we'll see in Chapter 5. Therefore, it makes sense to do whatever you can to build a positive team.

To what extent is your team positive at the moment?

Not at all	Slightly	To some extent	Fairly	To a great extent

To what extent are you confident that you actually know?

Not at all	Slightly	To some extent	Fairly	To a great extent

Honest reflection

If your answer is anything less than "to a great extent", you need to act.

Consider what the reasons *might be* for the negative atmosphere. Your understanding of the situation could be different to other people's.

If you are not a leader yet, reflect honestly on the causes of any negativity in the team you are in, and whether or not your leaders are aware of it.

As a leader, are you confident about what you know?

If you do have a positive team, be pleased with this but identify why it is the case.

Why is the mood positive? How can you be confident in your appraisal of the situation?

As in most work situations, you get the best response when you lead by example. If you come across as upbeat and ready to have a go at anything with a smile, then your team are more likely to follow. The best place to start is with the professional relationships you have with your colleagues. Your aim should be to build a culture in which your led colleagues do what you ask them to do because they want to. They are not merely compliant; they are committed to your cause. This is very difficult to achieve in a negative atmosphere. If your team trust you and you display integrity, commitment will naturally follow. It is very difficult to feel negative about someone who you trust to do the right thing. You need to foster a working environment in which colleagues feel that they can come to you at any time to talk about their work. Approachable is something we want all our leaders to be.

If there is negativity, you need to find out why. Ask:

- What are the challenges of working here?
- What can I do to make things better?
- If you were in my position, what would you do to improve things?

How often have you been asked these questions by a leader?

Never	Seldom	Sometimes	Regularly	Very often

Honest reflection

Look at your response. How much impact does being consulted have on your motivation and general attitude towards your work?

Think about your previous schools. If you can identify different responses for different workplaces, can you note the effects that each school had on you?

If you can see a cause and effect, take this with you and apply it to your leadership work.

A problem you could face is colleagues' dissatisfaction coming from something that is beyond your direct control – for example, an initiative imposed by a more senior colleague. This is a proper middle leadership challenge. If we are completely honest, there will be times when we don't agree with what we have to apply but are under strict instruction to make it happen.

One way in which you can address this is to show empathy towards your led colleagues. Let them know that you understand their problems and concerns. This is where being a hands-on leader really helps. You will be experiencing the same issues and cannot be accused of being in an ivory tower.

As we will see in Chapter 5, it can be very dangerous to overlook the perils of not changing. If you tell your colleagues about why a new strategy is needed and the consequences of not going along with it, then you will be making the change easier for people to accept. However, it is still good to be honest with them and admit that it is not easy for you either. Let your team know that you understand their position.

How often have you had a leader admit that the going will be tough?

Never	Seldom	Sometimes	Regularly	Very often

How often have you had a leader tell you to "just get on with it"?

Never	Seldom	Sometimes	Regularly	Very often

Honest reflection

How did you react to:

- The honest admission that things would be tough?
- Being told to "just get on with it"?

Your reaction to these situations is important. Were you motivated to work harder and get involved? Or the opposite?

Think about how your reflections can influence your strategies as a middle leader.

The cohesive team

In my experience, people tend to work better for individuals they like. Some of the best years of my working life have been in places where nearly everyone got on well. As a team leader, you need to work as hard as you can to be liked by your colleagues. Try to develop positive relationships, but do not confuse this with trying to be everyone's friend. That is completely different and not a very good idea.

It goes back to what we've already covered: be trustworthy, fair, approachable and reliable. Be these things and it will be hard to dislike you.

Case study

"We had a very difficult character on the staff. He was aggressive and always looking for an argument. In fact, I think the previous head of department left because of his goings-on. It definitely had an effect on the whole team's morale. Although it wasn't easy, I made the point of not reacting to him in the same way. I stayed calm, let him know he could come and sound off at any time … just reassured him that I'd think about his grumbles. I can't honestly say he changed massively, but it seemed to defuse things and the mood lifted a lot. He didn't seem to dislike me as much as he did my predecessor. I think that helped."

Jules, head of English

How your team develops

Bruce Tuckman's theory of small team development is well established. There are hundreds of links online, but I prefer Peter Levin's (2004: 77–78) summary. It is worth looking at. I refer to four of Tuckman's stages, ranging from when the team is first formed up to the time when the team is performing well and its mission has been met. As you read through the stages, think about examples that you have experienced in your teams.

Stage 1: Forming

The first stage is when everyone is still settling in. Team members try to find out about one another and the work involved. People test the ground with regards to the rest of the team and what they will be doing. This is the time when relationships start to be built between all levels within the team.

Although this sounds like it only applies to the formation of a brand-new team, it's not always the case. The forming stage will also happen when you have a new team member arriving. They might be replacing someone who has been with you for years. You can imagine how the dynamics of a group can change. Will there be a new formal or informal hierarchy? Will individuals try to reposition themselves within the team? Will existing members still have the same responsibilities? What if you are the new person? There will inevitably be some form of relationship testing.

Stage 2: Storming

During this stage you can expect some degree of conflict. As team members get to know each other better, they become more vocal and confident about their input. Even in a well-established team, the arrival of someone new will trigger uncertainty. If you are the leader of an established team, you'll need to think about how to introduce a new member into the group. How that person is integrated following the forming stage is important. You'll need to manage the process carefully. You can't afford for this stage to last too long because it will interrupt the progress of your work.

One problem at this stage is if you have a new team member arriving halfway through a project. It can slow things down because of the pressures that are created when helping someone to fit in. What part are they going to play? What responsibilities will they have? Are they getting in the way of what people are doing? An important task for you as a team leader is to make sure that the new person doesn't come in and lecture everyone about what they should be doing.

Case study

"We were going through a period of poor behaviour. We had tried a lot of different things and taken a load of advice. Three of us had been on training courses and things. Then in comes Martine. At our first meeting, she's telling us what we should have done. She tells us about how great she was at her last place. On and on. The thing was, we'd done all the stuff she was on about. Then Josie kind of politely tells her to shut up and reels off the list. It put Martine in her place! We loved that! But there was a funny atmosphere for weeks after. All a bit awkward."

Martin, NQT

Stage 3: Norming

This is where things start to settle down. New working relationships are accepted, and some team members might take on new roles. Generally, the group dynamic is accepted. The best part is when team members start to feel that they can trust each other. Things start to get done. Although you might face tricky moments, a lot of teams can get back to this stage almost immediately. Some don't even notice any problems.

Stage 4: Performing

This stage is when everyone is completely settled (or as much as they can be). The task can be worked on efficiently because everyone knows their place in the structure and their expectations of each other are generally understood. The team's energy is channelled into the task: it isn't wasted on petty arguments or jostling for position.

You will hear about a fifth stage: adjourning. This is when the team has done its work and breaks up. We're not talking about teams set up for specific, short-term projects here, so we won't delve into this aspect.

This team development model makes it look like things will work out well in the end. There might be a few bumps along the way, but allow the process to flow and your team will be hard-working and trustworthy. They will be more likely to be fully committed to the projects you are working on. Unfortunately, this won't happen on its own. It is your role as a middle leader to make it so.

Motivating your colleagues

Outstanding leaders go out of their way to boost the self-esteem of their personnel. If people believe in themselves, it's amazing what they can accomplish.

Sam Walton, quoted in Ilya Pozin (2014)

When talking about motivation here, I mean getting your team to act in ways that benefit the school without disaffecting them as individuals. Teams need motivating and there will be times when this is a challenge. As a leader, you need the skills to address this. Start building these skills as soon as you can and get some practice utilising them early in your leadership career. This way you will have a very valuable resource for later.

Middle leadership is probably one of the first scenarios in which you will have to motivate adults in a formal situation. It is different to motivating a class of young people, although there are a lot of similarities. This can be tricky at the start of your leadership career because you could well find yourself leading a team that has more experience than you. Or, more accurately, they have been teaching for longer than you have. It is a fact of professional life that many will equate length of service with expertise. In my experience, this isn't guaranteed.

What is guaranteed is that when you are new to the school, everyone else will know more about the place than you do. Some might use this as a way of blocking any changes you want to make. Equally, they might want you to change something that your predecessor introduced.

Sooner or later, you will certainly find yourself having to introduce a directive from senior colleagues. You are the messenger, and we all know what can happen to them! In order to encourage your led colleagues to work with you and have the collective impact that you want, the way in which you motivate your team needs careful consideration. Having worked in nine schools and a university, I can assure you that the well-motivated teams that I was part of all had high morale. This manifested itself in colleagues being more engaged in their work and certainly more open to providing goodwill. Members of these well-motivated teams looked out for each other and their resilience was noticeable. This is a game changer.

This is a good time to look at some theory. In his hierarchy of human needs, American psychologist Abraham Maslow (1943) uses phrases that refer to recognition, reaching our full potential and having a sense of belonging. Peter Northouse (2015: 230), for example, points out that Maslow's hierarchy identifies "esteem and recognition" as needs. Northouse continues, "we want to feel significant, useful and worthwhile".

"Meaningful work" is also recognised. The challenge for you here will be that individuals in the team will have a different understanding of the term. Meaningful work plays a big part in motivation and job satisfaction.

Honest reflection

What are the aspects of your job that make it "meaningful"? Take time to consider this and plan to review your thoughts later in your career.

What aspects of your job do you consider to be the most meaningful?

Have these views changed as you have gained more experience?

It is very common for people to become demotivated if their work is too easy for them. The problem we have is that the demands of everyday teaching can be exhausting, so the thought of taking on other tasks can be daunting. Your led colleagues might like the idea of additional, interesting work but may not have the capacity to take it on. This is an issue that middle leaders have to address. The only way to find out how your led colleagues feel is to ask them. A good time is during one-to-one meetings when you are new in post. Colleagues will appreciate your interest in them. There will have to be some negotiation with senior leaders regarding workload allocation: you will not have the final say.

I know several teachers who have got stuck in a rut and become very disillusioned with the job. If there is no challenge or interesting work involved, there will be little satisfaction over time. This is important because a lot of negativity can be caused by colleagues who are able but unhappy.

Honest reflection

Can you think of any colleagues who seem to be constantly grumbling about the job?

Reflect on how much experience they have. What is their role?

What kind of influence do they have on the rest of the staff?

If you think these colleagues are demotivating the team, look at Chapter 7 for ways to approach them.

We all have different things that motivate us. However, research carried out by Teresa Amabile and Steven Kramer (2011) has identified some common ground, which all leaders should know about. They looked at "knowledge workers": those professionals who have to be "creatively productive" every day – a good fit for us. They identified what they called the "progress principle". Put simply, we are highly motivated by making progress in meaningful work. Interestingly, it was the non-leaders who reported that they were motivated by progress. The managers in the study thought that *recognition* was a key factor. So it is no great leap to put these factors together to create a solid idea about how to motivate your team: give your team members meaningful work and recognise their progress.

Honest reflection

Is the progress *you* have made at work recognised? Reflect on your reactions when you have been given recognition. Did it make you want to do more?

What about times when you felt that your efforts haven't been noted or appreciated. Has this demotivated you?

Identifying your personal relationship with recognition will help you to recognise its importance. You will be learning from the actions of other people.

Although I have come across a couple of leaders who enjoyed being feared, most want their colleagues to be happy working for them. As a middle leader, you will no doubt hope that led colleagues feel that way about you.

Honest reflection

You could ask colleagues the question: "If I moved schools, would you come and work for me again?"

Think of a leader you have worked with who you would happily work for again.

List the reasons why.

Do you have these attributes?

Also, think about the difference between being nice and being popular. Are there disadvantages to just being nice and friendly?

Copy and complete this table to reflect on the attributes you admire in your colleagues.

Current experience reflection activity			
Person	**Attribute/skill**	**Can I do this?**	**If yes, give some examples.** **If no, what do I need to do?**
Soraya. Humanities lead.	Always backs her team in public.	No.	Get to know the strengths of every team member.

Would you like yourself as a boss?

You need to make your school a place where people *want* to work. So how do we go about developing this environment from a middle leadership position? An increasing number of businesses are using "internal marketing" as a way of motivating, and therefore keeping, good staff. This is worth considering in the school environment.

Rosalind Masterson and David Pickton (2014: 513) have no doubts about what demotivates people:

- Lack of detail about the proposed changes.
- Not having the ability or the knowledge to do the work required.
- Having the skills, but not the personal drive.
- Having different priorities.

Pause here for a second and think about how you, as a middle leader, fit into this. What's the impact of the actions that your leaders take?

- Do you suffer from a lack of information from your senior leaders?
- How does this affect how well you do your work?
- Do you have the skills to carry out your role effectively?
- Have you had the training needed to do your job properly?

Honest reflection

Are you sure that you keep your colleagues informed? Prove it to yourself by listing the communication methods you use.

Next, ask your team how they rate the level of communication from you.

Have there been times when you've been frustrated by the lack of understanding of your expectations? If "yes", then why was this? What could you have done differently?

List the members of your team. Put a comment about their skill level next to each of their names. Do they have the skills necessary to perform their work effectively? Are there any gaps?

These reflections will help to inform you about how well you are allowing your team to work effectively.

The attitude of your team members is very important. To keep your colleagues motivated, consider these strategies:

- Encourage collaboration. Nobody can do this job of education on their own. Apply Kanter's "team up" advice, which we encountered in Chapter 3, and also look out for the effect size of "collective efficacy" on page 100.

- Make sure that there is support for led colleagues at *every* level. Value the work of everyone connected with your team. For example, TAs and learning support workers can get overlooked and this will demotivate them. The value of these colleagues is being questioned in some areas and I think this is because they are not being allowed to do the things that do have a positive impact. For example, I know of one school where a TA is regularly taken away from her targeted support role to supervise absent teachers' classes, which is not an effective use of her expertise.

- Recognise the most experienced people in your team by asking them to contribute to any decisions being made. Whilst we shouldn't confuse experience with guaranteed efficacy, this is an especially good strategy for overcoming resistance to change. Consider this when you read Chapter 5.

From the outset, communicate good news and progress. Newsletters, vlogs, blogs and message boards are very effective tools. Spreading this information will build a culture of motivation in your team. At a seminar at the University of Bristol, I heard Evernote's Dr Beat Bühlmann – general manager for Europe, the Middle East and Asia – talk about how they use a large whiteboard in their office (see also Fritzsche 2017). Here is a high-tech company that values colleagues writing things down for everyone else to see using a dry-wipe pen. You don't need cutting-edge technology to keep getting the message across, as long as you provide access to information as frequently as possible.

The school might have performance-based incentives in place, so use these if it is allowed. If you are new to the school, ask about these early on. You can also come up with some of your own. There might be opportunities to delegate more responsibility or authority. This could be asking a colleague who you lead to take your place at a subject conference and then run a staff meeting linked to it. You'll certainly have to watch out for workload and pay issues, but I can clearly remember the first time I was asked to do this. It undoubtedly enhanced my status in school, and I was very grateful to the head of department. I was willing to go the extra mile after that.

Case study

"Primary schools in our local authority used to go on a residential trip to Devon in the summer term. The camp ran over about eight weeks and your school would share the facilities with three or four others for one of the weeks. In the spring term there was a meeting for all of the schools going. Each sent a representative to the meeting to sort out duty rotas and the like. The first time I was asked to do this I was very pleased. In fact, I can remember being excited by the prospect. An afternoon away from the class doing a job on behalf of the school. It doesn't seem much now, but I clearly relished the trust."

Deb, PE coordinator

Make sure that you send messages to members of your department/key stage/ age phase that are specific to them. For example, messages to teachers might be different to messages aimed at IT support staff. By doing this you will show that you understand and value the unique role that they play in the team.

▨ Have a clear idea of what led colleagues think about the aspect of school life that you are running. Try to have regular meetings with colleagues to find out if they are happy with the way things are going and what they need in order to carry out their work effectively. This is essentially about knowing your team. As Irvine and Brundrett (2016: 90) quote from a participant in their research, knowing your team:

> *"is fundamentally one of the most crucial things in the job ... if you don't under-stand the people you work with, they will pick it up, and it won't work as a team."*

Treating others as we would expect to be treated ourselves – a lesson from the corporate world

H. V. MacArthur (2019), writing for *Forbes*, states:

> *So how do companies stay competitive and not only retain employees but inspire candidates to commit to their mission and work of the company? [...] Treat them like customers.*

School leaders at every level should ask themselves if they are doing this. It is another example of internal marketing and recognises that employers must invest heavily in employee quality and performance.

How are we expected to treat our "customers"?

Masterson and Pickton (2014: 282) categorise teaching as being in the service industry: a product "that has no physical form". They go on to suggest that people judge service industry products as a whole. If you look at travel review websites, you will find many examples of this. It is not uncommon for restaurants, even where the food is good, to be given one-star reviews because of slow service and surly staff. Customers are judging the whole experience.

For us, this means it's not just about test and exam results but things like how we present ourselves at parent consultation evenings and open days, and the welcome parents get when phoning or dropping into the school with a concern. This needs to be extended to how leaders present themselves to members of their teams.

How do we treat our team members?

If teachers are expected to treat parents, carers and students with respect, then leaders need to convey this level of civility to team colleagues. For this to work, it follows that as a middle leader you need to master using your interpersonal skills with staff. Build this into your set of skills now and it will pay back in the future when you are in more senior positions. We are back in Chapter 2 and dispositions territory again.

Honest reflection

How are the staff in your school expected to treat parents and carers? Consider things like communication, politeness, a welcoming approach and how they explain decisions and actions.

How do you extend these courtesies to your team?

Do senior staff treat you in the same way?

If there are areas of weakness here, address them.

If you are not treated particularly well by senior colleagues, think about how this makes you feel and use this to influence how you treat your team.

Delegation: its part in meaningful work

If you are giving people "meaningful work" this often means delegation. I understand delegation as the act of giving a level of responsibility and control of specific work to a led colleague.

The problem is, a lot of us find delegating quite difficult, especially in the early days of our leadership careers. But why is this so?

I have no shame in reflecting on my own situation. To start with, I found it almost impossible to delegate. My first experience of genuine delegation came when I was a deputy head. I was worried that if a colleague failed to do the work that I had asked them to do, it would reflect badly on me. It was easier to keep doing a lot of tasks myself. The result was overload: hardly a surprise. I would have been far better off learning how to delegate. This is why delegation is hard: you still have the accountability but less of the control. It's an awkward situation and one that can get tougher the higher up the ladder you go.

If you have just taken over a team, everyone will already have their delegated tasks. Find out if they are happy to keep doing them. After a while, you might want to change things around, but only do this with agreement and having discussed the details with those involved.

Case study

"I'd had the CPD [continuing professional development] budget responsibility for years. Then the new head arrived and decided to take it away from me. He didn't give me a reason to start with. I was very disappointed about it. It made it look like I couldn't do the job. He explained later. He wanted to have a clearer understanding of all the cost centres, so took them on himself. Interesting. A sort of backwards delegation! Later on, he asked me if I wanted to have the responsibility back. I told him to **** off."

Kyle, assistant head, large primary school

A lot of things will be going through your mind when you first start to delegate. It is natural to worry about the outcome. Don't forget, you got the promotion because of your reputation. You know how to perform well. This makes it difficult because you might have doubts over whether your led colleague can do the job as well as you could. However, it is ridiculous to think that you can hold a leadership position without some level of delegation. What you must do is take an honest stock of what you do and be clear about your senior colleagues' expectations of your role. How do your leaders organise their work? Ask yourself: does the principal do break duty every day, teach 20 lessons a week, run an after-school activity and then carry out all their leadership responsibilities? Probably not. Other people are asked to do things to reduce the load. No one can do it all. It is very obvious, and basic common sense, but a lot of new leaders still find it difficult.

You need to ease your way into delegation. If you have a new colleague who is yet to have work delegated to them, start with something fairly easy. This will not only help build their confidence, but it will also build your confidence in them. Although this sounds simplistic, it serves another purpose, as you do not want to take too many risks when delegating for the first time. If one of the first tasks you delegate fails badly, and the implications are serious, you are unlikely to want to delegate again any time soon.

It is important to match the task to the colleague. There is a time and a place for taking people out of their comfort zone and your early days probably isn't it. So, find work that is challenging enough to be rewarding without being outright terrifying.

Making sure that you're using their strengths rather than putting them in a situation where it's their weaknesses that come out. (Irvine and Brundrett, 2016: 90)

Be careful, though. Very able colleagues will not like to be patronised. If you see a new colleague performing well, move them on to more challenging work. Tell them how well they've done and make your appreciation clear.

There is a concern that not many of us will admit to having. What if the person we delegate to does a really good job? So good that they look better than us?! Although this sounds bizarre, you'll find people in every profession who like to be seen as the best performer, and teaching is no different. I have worked with several. However, don't let this worry you. It is sensible to want your colleagues to perform delegated tasks well. It will reflect well on you. Use their success as recognition of your leadership skills. This is a common approach and you see it a lot in schools where they pride themselves on how many staff move on through promotion. They take credit for their colleagues' success. This is a good attitude to develop.

In order for colleagues to perform their delegated tasks well, they will need the tools to be able to do the job. If there are strategies that you have used successfully, pass them on to your colleagues. It is worth remembering that you will still be held accountable for any problems, so do your best to make sure that things don't go wrong. You will not want to be seen as interfering, so build in some regular, informal discussion points. That said, be aware that different people will have fresh ways of doing things. Although you might have given your colleague all the tools and guidance they need, they might want to do things their own way. Don't block their enthusiasm by insisting that yours is the only way. If their idea is very different then it will need monitoring. If it works well, then give yourself the credit for allowing it to happen and congratulate them on their success.

If you delegate well, the benefits to you will be substantial. Giving colleagues tasks that have become everyday practice for you – but that will stretch them – will free you up to engage in things that you'll find more interesting. It is often the unchallenging tasks which mount up that cause overload. In fact, you will be able to do things that are more meaningful at your level. Then if your colleague performs well, you can take credit for facilitating this and get recognition. Both you and the delegated-to colleague will be in the position of being praised for successfully carrying out meaningful work.

Concluding thoughts

Leading your team effectively will result in positive outcomes. It is worth putting the time and effort into making sure it's done properly.

Try to take shortcuts here and you'll only make life difficult for yourself.

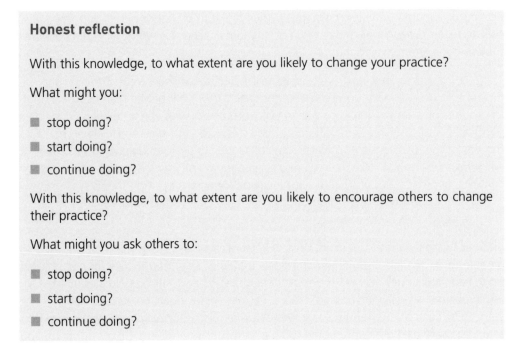

Honest reflection

With this knowledge, to what extent are you likely to change your practice?

What might you:

- stop doing?
- start doing?
- continue doing?

With this knowledge, to what extent are you likely to encourage others to change their practice?

What might you ask others to:

- stop doing?
- start doing?
- continue doing?

Chapter 5

Leading Change: Where Your Leadership Ability Is Judged

Ordering people to change and then telling them how to do it fires the prefrontal cortex's hair trigger connection to the amygdala. The more you try to convince people that you're right and they're wrong, the more they push back. The brain will try to defend itself from threats.

David Rock (2006)

By the end of this chapter, you should have a clear idea of the challenges involved in running a change project and an understanding of some of the strategies needed to make it work.

As I was researching this chapter and reflecting on my own experience, it became very apparent that the same issues repeat themselves with surprising regularity. There is considerable overlap in the content that follows, and this goes to show how often leaders are making the same mistakes, repeatedly.

This raises the question:

How often do you consider your behaviour around leading change?

Never	Seldom	Sometimes	Regularly	Very often

Making changes is a major part of leadership and management. Although you will be spending a lot of time managing existing practices, the time will come when you need to take on a change project. Change is very often needed as a result of pressures from both inside and outside the school. The triggers can range from fairly minor events to critically important insights, and leading these changes will be some of the most important work you do as a leader. How you go about this will be noticed by everyone around you. It will be how you are remembered. It will be the benchmark against which you are judged. Your reputation as a leader will be built on this aspect of your work.

Why change anything?

The reason for introducing a change project is to move your school from where it is now to a place where it can reach its objectives more effectively. To make this happen, you must have a clear idea of the gap between the starting point and the desirable conclusion. You must tell your colleagues about the *legitimate reasons* for the change and, at all costs, avoid change for the sake of change.

The five things you don't want colleagues to ask

When you introduce a change project to your team, there are five questions you don't want them to ask:

1.   Why are we doing this?

2.   What are we expected to do?

3.   Where do we stand in the process?

4.   Who's in charge?

5.   Have we got the skills to do it?

This chapter is about how to make these points clear before the questions are raised.

Use change cycles

You will find a lot of "change cycle" examples online. With any theory or suggested model, it is common practice to choose components from those that suit us best. This means a personal, hybrid version evolves. The one I summarise here is an amalgamation of many common approaches but has its roots in a model that I was introduced to during the Access Stage of the NPQH back in 2001. Whichever model you use, make sure that it will help to answer those five awkward questions before anyone has the chance to ask them. These steps need to be covered.

1. Have a precise picture of what the problem is and tell your team

Don't be too vague. For example, "poor behaviour" is too general to act upon effectively. "Year 9 transition from break time to next lesson is poor, especially in hallways" is better. Or ask key questions to get the precise detail.

Q: What is the behaviour issue that is causing us most concern?

A: Break time.

Q: Is it general or more specific?

A: Upper Key Stage 3.

Q: What does the bad behaviour look like?

A: It starts off OK, but they get very unruly towards the end.

This type of questioning will help identify areas that can be more easily dealt with because you and your team are not wasting time on things that might not need addressing – behaviour in lower Key Stage 3, for example.

This helps to answer question 1 – "Why are we doing this?"

2. Gather clear evidence of how well you are doing

It is no good only having anecdotal evidence. Produce written evidence following observation. For example, "I've heard that Year 4s don't do any extended writing" lacks authority. "Following the last work scrutiny, we noticed that only some of the most able children were being given the chance to write longer pieces." There can be no argument here.

This helps to answer question 1.

3. Find out how you compare with other schools/departments

This will give you some real benchmarks. For example, "I think we can have better interactive displays than this" is your opinion, but based on what? "When we were over at Town Street Academy for the INSET day last week, I noticed these displays [shows photographs for evidence]. This is what we need to be doing." This will inevitably prompt some colleagues to say how different your school is and so you can't compare. Don't let this excuse put you off.

This helps to answer question 1.

4. Investigate *what* they are doing that makes them better than you

Find out from colleagues at Town Street Academy how they have such effective displays. Then see if you can apply similar strategies. This will provide you with a good model.

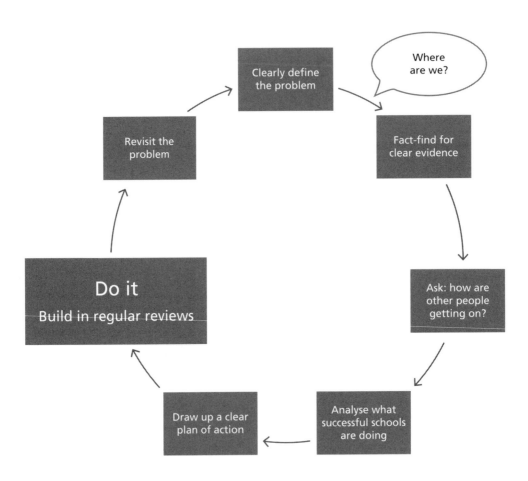

Discussing the details with colleagues from the other school will help identify the challenges that they had to address.

This helps to answer question 1 and question 2 – "What are we expected to do?"

5. Draw up a plan of what you need to do to improve

Use the evidence that you have gathered and shared with your colleagues. Set out a clear timetable that includes dates for monitoring and feedback meetings. Identify any areas where staff will need training and support (which often translates as "we need more time to do the work"). Allocate clear tasks to staff. Manage the budget.

This helps to answer question 2, question 3 – "Where do we stand in the process?" – and "question 4 – "Who's in charge?" Crucially, it will help to address question 5 – "Have we got the skills to do it?"

6. Take action

Start working through the plan and stick to the timings as closely as possible. Never miss an opportunity to share a success. Never ignore or dismiss any problems. Communication is vital.

Publicly recognising success will have a very positive effect, making everyone believe that, in answer to question 5, yes, they have got the skills.

7. Review step 1

Gather evidence to see if the problem still exists or if it has improved in some way. If things still aren't where you want them to be, go through the process again. This is where any training needs often get uncovered and budget issues come to light.

Barriers

Leading change would be very simple if all we had to do was follow a cycle. Be prepared for challenges along the way. The culture of any workplace can be difficult to shift. The most frustrating words to hear from colleagues are: "This is the way we do things around here. We've always done it this way." Change can be hard to accept, which is why colleagues need to know exactly why something new is being introduced. The project can be something major – for example, a new marking policy for your subject area, implementing a new curriculum or introducing a restructured behaviour management policy

– or it might be something less crucial that blends in to support other developments – for example, your subject area's contribution to a new whole-school policy on reporting to parents and carers.

Northouse (2015: 128) argues that whilst change is inevitable, it is important for leaders to be "socially perceptive". By not understanding the significance of a proposed change, we can cause ourselves a lot of unnecessary problems. He uses the example of the University of Michigan having to change the venue used for its graduation ceremonies. University leaders decided to hold the ceremonies at Eastern Michigan University. This caused huge protests, with graduates and their families finding the new venue "offensive". To correct the situation, the university found a place back on their own campus to hold the event. This was well-received. As Northouse suggests, had leaders been more socially perceptive, the dissatisfaction could have been avoided. I can only imagine the anxiety that those decision makers felt. As a middle leader in charge of a change project, the pressure is on you to make it succeed, so don't put up unnecessary barriers.

The sustainability of change is always a problem. Making your change project stick will require effort and careful consideration. You need to find ways of minimising the stress of the process. There is a lot of well-established advice in leadership theory, but it is alarming to see how often it is ignored. It is worth preparing yourself with an insight into what people commonly say when resisting change. Kanter (2012) distils a lot of what's been written into key points. I have chosen the ones that most affect us and added an educational leadership context to each.

See which of these could be addressed by using the strategies noted previously.

1. "This didn't work last time we did it."

This is the first on the list because it is the objection that I've heard the most. You'll get this from experienced colleagues. Things tend to go in and out of fashion – and back again – with surprising regularity. For example, you might hear: "We did this ten years ago. It failed then, so it probably will now." Or: "We used to assess in this way before and it was fine. But we were told it was rubbish by the last head teacher and had to throw everything out. Years of hard work wasted … and now you're bringing it back! No chance!"

Not only will you meet resistance, but it will make you look foolish. Do your research. Find out from colleagues if anything similar has been tried and failed in the school. If it has, don't be put off if you think it is worthwhile. However, if you introduce your change project by recognising that it has similarities with initiatives that have been tried – and failed – in the past, you will avoid some of the derision. If you can identify the shortcomings that the previous attempt had, so much the better. And don't forget, the context is different now. Some of the evidence that these sceptics provide will be out of date or will have been exaggerated over time.

Suggestion: In your teaching, you probably use *predictive intervention.* The ability to spot our students' potential misunderstandings can improve our impact considerably. So why not apply this to your leadership practice? See if you can predict what the objections to your change project might be.

To be fair, our colleagues could have had bad experiences of frequent imposed change in the past. This is very true in a lot of schools due to the external pressures they are under. In this case, it is a good idea to find out what happened and ask their opinion about what made it a bad project. This will get them involved. The next step is to ask them to contribute to your proposed project "in order to help you learn from past mistakes". Although I wouldn't give your colleagues a checklist like the one on pages 89–90, it will be good information gathering for you. Structure a conversation in order to fill it in yourself. Use the past tense and ask questions like: "What were you trying to achieve?" and "Did you have the right people in the team?"

You are asking them to help make this change project a success. You are showing them that you trust their professionalism, and they will have invested some time and effort into it. This activity will clearly highlight colleagues' *perceptions*, so even if they are not wholly correct, it will steer you towards strategies that work.

2. "How will this affect me?"

In the time leading up to a proposed change, we are often happy with the way things are going. Even if we are not completely satisfied, we can be confident in our ability to do the tasks and in our understanding of what colleagues' expectations are. When all this looks like it's going to change, that confidence can be lost very easily.

When you are the leader imposing the change, it is important to realise that your colleagues will sense a loss of control over their work. When tasks that have become second nature look like they are disappearing, the independence that your led colleagues feel will also be under threat. Colleagues who have the confidence to do so will ask how the change will affect them. Don't be afraid of this. Encourage them to ask as many questions as they want to because this will help you to focus on some of the finer detail that you might have missed. Use their questions to build your understanding of their concerns. This, in turn, will add to your authority.

Suggestion: Give those who are affected by the change the chance to make choices. Invite them to planning meetings and monitoring sessions. Giving ownership is a tried and tested strategy for challenging resistance. This is probably the most common advice that trainers and leadership experts give.

3. "I haven't got a clue what's happening."

Kanter (2012) suggests that if the incoming change feels like "walking off a cliff blind-folded", then people will reject it. She goes on to say: "People will often prefer to remain mired in misery than to head toward an unknown." This might seem ridiculous, but it certainly happens. It is your responsibility as a leader to make the details of the change very clear to your colleagues. From the outset, the benefits of the project need to be made obvious to everybody.

Suggestion: Be very open about how things are progressing. Build in checkpoints and look for team members to be part of the monitoring process. Don't leave it too long between feedback meetings but try not to overload the process. It's about getting the balance. Listen to what colleagues are saying. Are they making comments about not knowing what's going on or grumbling about your fixation with your pet project?

Build in opportunities for colleagues to report back on the progress they are making. This way they are part of the communication process and are less likely to say that they don't know what's going on. This type of two-way communication can be done virtually, through email or the school's virtual learning environment (VLE) or using productivity tools that bring groups together. Ayoa (previously called DropTask) and Evernote are examples of these.

4. "We weren't expecting this!"

Kanter (2012) advises leaders to avoid making the change project a surprise. Again, openness is regarded as important. She adds: "Leaders should avoid the temptation to craft changes in secret and then announce them all at once." If you surprise your colleagues with something, it gives them little chance to think about the consequences and how to prepare. This will lead to resistance and the probability that your project won't take off well. How can we be expected to give our attention and energies to something that has come out of the blue? At times it is simple uncertainty of the unknown, but consider this: if you try to impose a strategy that is seen as a knee-jerk reaction, would you be surprised to see a knee-jerk reaction in response?

Obviously, there will be times when a change needs to be made quickly. Anything to do with child safety is a good example of this. A poor inspection outcome is another. You won't have much time to ponder over the details if you are judged as requiring improvement or worse. However, it is still important to get your team together and tell them what to expect. Again, getting their opinions is worthwhile. Realistically, if you have had a disappointing inspection report, everyone will be expecting action. Be swift, thoughtful and open.

Suggestion: In the normal run of things, try not to surprise your led colleagues. It is a good idea to start indicating that some changes might need to be made in the future to prepare the ground for a new initiative. Let your team know what you have in mind and invite them to make initial comments.

I know of several schools where the leaders have introduced several changes very quickly, surprising their colleagues. It builds an atmosphere in which staff go to meetings wondering if another bombshell is going to be dropped. This is a mistake because it takes away the impact you need when something is genuinely urgent.

5. "I'm confused – *nothing* is the same."

We take comfort from following established routines but this calm, professional flow will be disrupted if too many things are changed at once. This will have a negative effect on outcomes. Whilst applying new strategies, try to keep some things familiar. Too much unfamiliarity will increase stress levels and could lead to the rejection of your change project. At the very least, you can expect a drop in the level of your colleagues' commitment.

For example, you might want to change the assessment gathering processes in the early years. It is a big undertaking but is desperately needed. However, you have been told at a leadership meeting that work needs to be done on planning formats and every class teacher has to be part of a trial. This will mean more work and creates yet another area in which your colleagues could be feeling unsure of what to do.

Another competing change project could be something completely different. You might want to introduce a specific marking policy for your department to fit your subject's needs. At the same time, tutor group protocols are being changed. This will have a big effect on your team members with tutor groups, and you will need to consider their workload. A thoughtful middle leader will be very aware of wider school issues and be sensitive about developments in other departments or key stages. Be conscious of changes being made in other areas that impact on your team. Use this awareness to manage the timing of any change project.

Suggestion: Don't introduce a change project at the same time as another, especially if the other is a whole-school initiative decreed by senior leaders. Plan to implement your changes as soon as colleagues have got to grips with the first steps of the whole-school project.

6. "This makes me look bad."

Any time change is suggested, it is likely that some colleagues will take it as a criticism of how things were done before, which is challenging, especially if they played a part in setting up the previous practices or were openly supportive of them. Avoid making colleagues feel bad about their work by highlighting how effective the old strategy was *at the time*. Then you need to establish why things need to move on. Emphasise that their effective practice is well-embedded.

A good leadership disposition is being able to understand how colleagues might be feeling and thus recognise their defensiveness. Admitting that you can see why they feel as they do will help soften the blow and make moving on easier.

Suggestion: Make it clear that the previous work has served its purpose well. Locate evidence from data, reports or inspections that state the positive impact at the time. You don't want to encourage colleagues to use this as an excuse to not change, so don't lose sight of the reasons for moving on. Emphasise your confidence in the team's ability to develop, "We've done it before, so let's repeat our success."

7. "Have I got the skills?"

Doubt is something that we all experience. You have been very happy with your work in a particular area. You've had no complaints and you've been seen as a very skilled practitioner. Then a change comes along. If you don't think you have the skills to continue at the same high level as before, then you are bound to feel threatened. In order to keep the level of respect that you have earned, you will probably want to resist the change.

Case study

"I have always enjoyed standing at the front of the class doing whole-class lessons. I suppose it is my chance to perform. People say that I am very engaging. That's nice. It shows I can motivate the children. They enjoy it too. Anyway, my boss went on a course and came back with this idea that the teacher shouldn't be 'the sage on the stage, but the guide on the side'. I'm worried about being graded badly, but I'll stand up for myself if I get into too much trouble because we've had no training."

Pia, Year 5 teacher

You can understand Pia's concerns. She's been regarded as a good teacher for years but now she doesn't think she'll be able to work in the "new" way. Conflict might occur if she raises the fact that she should have been given some training.

As a leader, think very carefully about the effect your changes could have on team members. The better you know your individual colleagues, the more chance you will have of making your changes work. Upset and frighten your colleagues and you'll find their resistance difficult to crack. This doesn't confine itself to complex pedagogical issues. I remember when one school I worked in first introduced electronic registers. We had several colleagues who refused to use them. Panic set in. Luckily, we had time to train everyone before implementing them, but it showed how worried people get if they think they'll be seen as incompetent.

Suggestion: Be honest. Tell your team that it's natural for them feel threatened, that you understand but that it is nothing to worry about. Offer coaching and training from the outset or, even better, before the change project starts. Show the team that you have confidence in their ability to learn new skills.

8. "It'll mean more work."

Change can mean more work, even if the outcome is intended to cut workload. It will probably mean more work for you, as a middle leader. Whether you're implementing an imposed change within your team or designing and evaluating your own change project, you will be exposed to the pressures of it not going to plan. But don't forget Kanter (2013), who says that everything can seem like a failure when you're halfway through. You need to acknowledge the effort that your team are putting into this work. Refer back to Chapter 4 for ideas. Often a small token of your appreciation can go down well.

Suggestion: Recognise what colleagues are saying, and tell them that you appreciate their input. A big mistake is to ignore these kinds of comments. You must recognise and address resistance. If you don't, things will only get worse and you are likely to see your project fail.

Colleagues who try to block change

A lot of us will know the characters who like nothing more than to disrupt anything that looks like change. In their e-book, *Accelerating Change Management: Getting 7 Personalities on Board*, project management company Wrike (2018) pick out who these characters are likely to be. You are likely to recognise some of these:

- Colleagues who exaggerate how badly things have gone in other schools because of too much change.

- Those who will try to find as much evidence as they can to prove how well things have gone before. They are likely to seek the support of colleagues who think in the same way. They certainly won't be interested in any evidence that contradicts them. This *confirmation bias* is often accompanied by bitterness. It can seem like certain colleagues are primed for confrontation. It is your job to present them with a clear argument about what needs to be changed and why.

- The masters of asking "why". They will quickly identify anything that is a waste of time. Often, these colleagues will let you think that everything is perfectly fine and working well as it is. Why bother changing things?

- The "know-alls". These are the ones I have had most problems with, as they don't care very much about the thoughts of other team members. They have their opinions on how things should be done and think they know best, and make sure that everybody knows it. This can lead to a falling-out with anyone who doesn't agree with their view.

Suggestion: Once you have identified someone who falls into any of these categories, you need to have some one-to-one meetings. If they have the chance to have a rant and offload to you, there's less chance that they'll do so in front of others. It's a good idea to ask them what their specific fears are and address them together. When you talk to them:

- Have examples of how things have worked well in different schools, departments or age phases. This is where networking with colleagues in different schools can be very useful. Real-life examples from across the MAT, alliance, partnership or local area work well.

- Show them evidence that opposes their entrenched views.

- Show them the planned evaluation timetable.

▓ Give them solid reasons for the change. You won't have to look too far for justification. The education world moves at a rapid pace. Schools are sometimes volatile places to work, with the need for change coming from different directions. In UK schools, the driving force is often inspection. Prompts for change might come from a national initiative or from an internal recognition that something needs to be done differently.

▓ Reiterate the reason for the change. Make it explicit. Show them the plan. Get them to contribute.

These points can be seen in the change cycle which we looked at earlier in this chapter, but to reinforce the message, have a look at Tim Hannagan's (2007) advice on how to lead a successful change project, adapted from *Management: Concepts and Practices*:

▓ Have a *vision* so that everyone knows where they are going.

▓ Have a *strategy* so that everyone knows how to get there.

▓ Keep *monitoring* progress to identify where we are now.

▓ Be *coherent* and find agreement on the operational tasks and goals which are consistent with the strategic view.

▓ Keep *communicating* clear and appropriate information.

▓ Create a clear *structure* and move logically through the process.

▓ *Do not ignore resistance* to change because this will only encourage it and make the feelings run deeper.

Follow this guidance and you'll stand a good chance of success.

The right questions to ask the right people

It is easy to talk about getting the right information, but in practice it is good to have a set of defined questions. Phil Wood (2017) from the University of Leicester put together some key questions that help to make change sustainable, which I have adapted. Cover these and you won't go far wrong.

What is the work about?

Be clear about the project's aims. Colleagues *must* know what the work is about. Tell your team what is new and what the benefits are. Establish whether they share your purpose. Do they see the point? Are they onboard? If not, find out why.

Who's doing what?

Wrike (2018) states that for effective change, you need *buy-in* from everyone affected by the change. They must understand, agree and commit to the proposed changes. Your job is to decide who needs to be involved and at what level. In middle leadership, you are likely to want all of your team to commit. This will look different at senior leadership level because there will be times when a change project won't apply to everyone – issues relating to a specific key stage, for example.

In your team there are likely to be members who can drive the change forward better than others. They will have the experience and know-how that colleagues will respect. They are invaluable in the early phases.

Case study

"Rachel totally understood the idea of layered targets. She built them into her work effortlessly. So, when it came to getting everyone to do this kind of work, I asked her to bring some examples along to a staff meeting. She was the perfect choice to get things going."

Rick, head teacher, small primary school

Take care to consider what the relationship dynamics are like. Is there anyone who might need coaching to be a genuine team player? In Rick's school, Rachel could be seen by one or two people as being too keen to please. Be aware of potential jealousy, and think about how some colleagues might need to be helped to overcome this. Senior colleagues should be able to tell you about appropriate policies and practices that have worked for them. A good strategy is to openly share ideas and encourage discussion, rather than blindly impose a particular person's contributions.

How are we going to get things done?

See if any training is needed. Are there some colleagues who need more than others? Workload is a hot topic. Make sure tasks are allocated fairly and seriously consider how you are going to support your individual colleagues. This is an ideal time for a SWOT analysis. Do an audit of the resources you have and see what else you need. A poorly resourced change project is unlikely to get very far. A discussion with colleagues who deal with the finances is essential.

How are we getting on? Does everyone understand what we're doing?

Reporting success is a great motivator, so think about how you are going to monitor progress. Some things are easier to track than others. Data analysis and work scrutiny will be effective, if done properly. Lesson observation is another well-established tool but try not to overdo this. Bear in mind how many observations are being carried out by different colleagues. You will get the best results if you use these techniques as a way of monitoring the progress of the change project, not as a way of checking up on the people working on it. Be honest and open with your team about what you are doing.

You need to find out from your team how *they* think things are going. Keeping an informal dialogue open is an effective strategy because it encourages conversations which provide the sort of detail that can be missed in formal settings such as staff meetings. As you gather information, always be receptive to changes that you might need to make. Your team will react well if they can see that their comments lead to modifications. You are valuing their input by acting on it.

It is important for you to have these points at the front of your mind. Think about a change project that you are going through or planning. Run through the following questions and note your responses.

- What are we trying to achieve?
- Can we clearly state our success criteria?
- How is this strategy different to what is already in place?
- Have we got the right people in the team? Do they need any training?
- Are we all heading in the same direction?
- What do we hope to gain?
- Can we resource the change project?

■ Have we got clear checkpoints in place?

■ Do the team members have the right information?

If your answer to any of these questions is "I don't know" or "No", take action.

Honest reflection

It is a worthwhile exercise to think about a change project that you have experienced in the past. You might have led it or been part of the team being led. Ideally, work with a colleague to answer these questions:

■ What was the change project and why was it put in place?

■ What could have been done better?

■ How would this have affected the result?

■ Which aspects went well?

■ How did these influence the success of the project?

By doing this, you will be able to see the effect of good practice. Make a note of the successes and add them to your portfolio of skills.

If you can see why some outcomes were not as good as expected, you can ensure that the mistakes are not made again.

Concluding thoughts

If you are prepared for objections to your change project and already have strategies in place to counter them, you stand a good chance of success. It is better to act pre-emptively before objections are raised.

Honest reflection

With this knowledge, to what extent are you likely to change your practice?

What might you:

- stop doing?
- start doing?
- continue doing?

With this knowledge, to what extent are you likely to encourage others to change their practice?

What might you ask others to:

- stop doing?
- start doing?
- continue doing?

Chapter 6

System Leadership from the Middle: A 21st Century Development

System leadership is defined as leaders who work within and beyond their individual organisations; sharing and harnessing the best resources that the system can offer ...

Ceri Matthias (2014)

By the end of this chapter, you should have an understanding of a middle leader's role in system leadership. Although David Hopkins' *The Emergence of System Leadership* was published in 2009, it is only more recently that it has become generally recognised, and it is still fairly new to schools. Fullan (2011) reports that a lot of work has already been done on this in Ontario, Canada, and we can learn a lot from their system structures. It's important for middle leaders to consider how the system leadership model will impact on their role.

Peter Clarke (2017), then of the National College for Teaching and Leadership (NCTL), which has since been disbanded, sees system leaders as those who "work beyond their own school or setting, and can be senior or middle leaders in schools or other expert practitioners". In England it is becoming more significant due to schools forming stronger alliances and partnerships amongst themselves. This can be in the form of MATs, teaching school alliances and less formal federations.

Although the wider, strategic aspect of system leadership remains the responsibility of senior leaders, middle leaders are increasingly required to move into a broader role. For example, as the maths leader in your school, your expertise might be regarded as valuable to others in the group. This will mean visiting other schools to pass on your knowledge. There will be a requirement for you to provide INSET across the group and follow this up by monitoring how your training has been applied. You are, in fact, acting as a consultant, and this requires a developed set of skills. Without doubt, when budgets are tight, you can expect more of this kind of work. In-house training is on the increase.

Since the 1990s, the system has seen advisory teachers, seconded local authority consultants and advanced skills teachers as well as lead teachers and school improvement partners. So, although in essence it is nothing new, system leadership now has more reach and structure than in the past. It is a 21st century development.

What new opportunities does it offer?

Peter Chilvers (2016), chief executive of the School Development Support Agency, sees it as a chance for "maturing leadership" with a different set of skills being needed as leaders widen their field of influence. Malcolm Trobe (2016), former interim general secretary of the Association of School and College Leaders (ASCL), saw new opportunities for subject leaders – middle leaders as we see them – to take on responsibilities across MATs. In the same vein, Chilvers hoped that more staff would be involved in this type of leadership, rather than just a "select group". The select group, I assume, being senior leaders. System leadership offers middle leaders a lot of opportunities to develop their leadership skills.

Where might this put you as a middle leader?

Effective system leaders can be at the forefront of potentially long-lasting change. If you develop this part of your work, you will be in a strong position to apply for more senior leadership positions later. To be a good system leader, you'll need to be able to see a bigger picture that goes beyond your school walls. You could have influence over how your subject is taught in several other schools, and the important aspects that go with it, such as assessment and planning. Also, it's very likely that you could be responsible for policy development in several schools.

This is a big shift in accountability, so if you find yourself being asked to take on a system leadership role, make sure you are getting the support you need from senior colleagues. It is essential that you are given the tools to do the job well. This should include:

▨ Structured support, including a mentor in your early days.

▨ An experienced line manager.

▨ Access to leadership resources – for example, lesson observation policies.

▨ A clear professional development plan.

▨ Realistic autonomy.

▨ Realistic accountability.

Before agreeing to take on a system leadership role, check that this support will be in place.

What will make it a success or not?

In *The Management Consultant: Mastering the Art of Consultancy*, Richard Newton (2010) uses the 4Cs to summarise what a good consultant should be: capable, competent, coherent and credible.

Of course, you'll likely already demonstrate these traits when carrying out your responsibilities in your own school. However, they will be amplified in a system leadership position. As a visiting system leader, it is vital that you add value to the school. You *must* add something to the school's performance. It could be showing colleagues an improved way of dealing with poor attendance or another non-class-based issue, or it could be advising them on how to make their jobs easier by adopting a new assessment strategy. Whatever the focus of your visit, think carefully about how to make sure that there is something in it for them.

Honest reflection

If you have ever had someone from another school come in to give training or offer advice, reflect on how much more you knew after they had gone.

- Did you find out something new?
- Was it relevant to you?
- Did you put this new information into practice?
- What was your general opinion of the visitor?

Record the positives and think about why this came about – for example, how did they know what you needed? Which of the 4Cs did they exhibit?

If there were any negatives, what were they?

Which of the 4Cs did they lack?

Consider this and you'll have a strong idea of people's expectations of you.

What makes an effective system leader?

Obviously, you'll want to be a successful system leader. Consider the blockers you might face and the enablers that you can use.

Success blockers

Negativity of colleagues

Newton believes that there is a difference between being good at something and being a good consultant. He develops an old joke: "Those who can, do; those who can't, teach; and those who can't teach, consult" (Newton, 2010: 21).

This criticism of consultancy is quite common in an education context. Some internet forums are full of similar comments from teachers. As a newly appointed local authority consultant in the 1990s, an experienced colleague told our team that there was only one thing likely to make you less popular than having "consultant" stamped on your forehead and that was "*local authority* consultant". Unfortunately, you might find this as a system leader when you work in different schools because there will be those who see you as an outsider. Often there is resistance from colleagues who will ask, "What do you know about our kids?" This can put you in a difficult spot, but we'll go into some suggestions to counter this in a moment.

What causes this animosity? Is it jealousy, distrust or resentment? There will always be colleagues who see all leaders as careerists but have an even deeper distrust of system leaders. In my opinion, some teachers justifiably feel that they are being unfairly criticised in the media and not respected by society as a whole. They then kick out against anyone who comes into their field of work, and colleagues from outside their school are looked at with suspicion. This isn't widespread, so don't let it worry you. Just be prepared: there are some suggestions to help listed as "enablers".

Poorly performing system leaders

Newton (2010) sets out what constitutes a poor consultant in both the private and public sectors. As you read the list, do you recognise any trainers or consultants who you've come across?

- Not enough real value given to the customers – teachers left wondering why someone has come in to tell them what they already know.

- Failure to fully understand the specific needs of the school/individual – the same generic content being churned out regardless of actual need.
- The consultant who thinks it is all about them – too much time is spent trying to be clever rather than addressing the issues that the school needs to address.

A poor understanding of the role

Peter Chilvers (2016) warns that colleagues who provide peer challenge within a system leadership context should not become "proxy inspectors". This can cause unimaginable negativity. Look back at Chapter 2. The way in which these things are done is important.

The selection of a visiting system leader needs to be carefully considered. In the business world, companies generally have a choice of consultant to hire. In a system-led education model, this isn't so clear-cut. It could well be someone from a school that is deemed to be performing better or a colleague who has specific expertise. As a local authority seconded consultant for assessment, my visits were imposed on the schools in the area. I arrived whether the school wanted me or not. Sometimes things were fine, other times they were difficult. What made the difference was how well-prepared the school was for my visit and how well I understood their needs. It was surprising how often I arrived to find that school colleagues were completely uninformed about my role and any expectations I had of them. Equally, I was sometimes sent to schools that didn't have any real need for my services. These scenarios could, and should, have been avoided by senior leaders being very clear about their requirements and making sure that the right people were invited to schools with identified needs at appropriate times.

Blockers will affect the sustainability of a system leader's work. If colleagues don't buy into it for any reason, progress will be slow.

Honest reflection

Have you ever been aware of colleagues criticising someone who has been delivering training at your school? It could be someone from outside the school, or a leader or colleague from a different part of your establishment.

- What sorts of comments did they make?
- What were they being negative about?
- Were they justified?

> ▣ When were they making the comments – before the event, during, after?
>
> By reflecting in this way, you will start to have an idea of what potential negativity you might encounter and be in a better position to address things *before* you start.

Enablers

The easiest way to identify enablers is to flip the blockers, but we need to add some extra layers.

High-performing system leaders who are recognised as such

Newton (2010) sets out what a good consultant should deliver. As noted, they *must* be adding value by making colleagues more effective, thus raising standards.

As a visiting system leader, you can do this by providing:

▣ **Independent advice.** As an outsider, with a good understanding of the school you are visiting, you can offer a different view of things. It can be something very subtle that perhaps the people who are too close to the organisation have not considered.

▣ **Recommendations to help apply the advice.** Suggestions for new strategies will be valued a lot more if you can guide your colleagues in applying it. A good way to do this is to offer to show people how it's done. An example might be a demonstration of a behaviour management technique that works for you – go into their school and show them how it works. This is very brave, but it will be appreciated a lot.

▣ **Skills and expertise.** As suggested previously, modelling your skills has a huge impact. Demonstrate your expertise by being quick to respond to questions and to counter any objections that might be raised. Supporting theory by giving examples of how you have approached the issue effectively works well, but don't overdo the anecdotes. It is not all about you, so give accounts of successful strategies that you have seen other colleagues use.

▣ **A clear dialogue with everyone involved that matches their specific needs.** This is very important. Getting to know the specific characteristics of the schools you are working in and everyone's individual needs will help address the assumption that "you don't know our students".

It is worth setting these points out as intentions at the start of your work. Colleagues should be in no doubt of the benefits of you being in their school, working alongside them. Do everything you can to allay their fears.

A clear understanding of role – knowing your place

The status a system leader has in their own school does not guarantee automatic respect in a different workplace. I was seconded as a local authority consultant from my day job as a deputy head. For some, this meant nothing; to others, it was all they needed to know, and trust soon developed. It is important for a system leader to recognise that their status won't just carry over, and that they will have to demonstrate their commitment to colleagues in other schools.

The advantage a system leader brings is having the positive attributes of both internal and external consultancy. Newton (2010) identifies the differences:

- The *internal* consultant will have a good understanding of the politics and culture of the institution.
- The *external* consultant will have wider experience, having worked in a variety of different settings and seen what works in varied circumstances.

This needs to be understood by the client school, so make it clear to them. Tell your audience what's in it for them.

Addressing negativity

Credibility is key. In the same way that good teachers model best practice to their students, a good system leader will give their colleagues examples of successes they have had in the focus area of the development programme. I have always appreciated an empathetic approach, which is soundly based on expertise gained through experience.

System leaders should be well informed, not just about the issue at hand, but about the context in which they are working. Being seen as the "expert" enhances perceptions of capability, which, in turn, builds the host school's confidence in the expert. Trust will get stronger when examples are given of how new strategies can be applied in the host school's environment. Think back to Chapter 3. The same rules apply, but for a wider audience.

You will want to be seen as someone who is trying to get to know the host school. Encourage reflection and comment from the group, then openly show respect for their views. Always encourage input from the group about their specific situation. This is a powerful way of establishing your competence: it cannot be underestimated. Clarke (2017) advocates this approach too, pointing out in his blog post the value of "individually tailored" school support. Work on developing this dialogue so that your input will be regarded as coherent and relevant. Get this right and no one can accuse you of being too generic.

The most successful system leaders are ones who are seen to clearly add value, whilst being a pleasure to work alongside. Following these principles of trust, commitment and expertise will help you to develop sustainable impact.

The impact of collaboration

Educational expertise is a product of exchange and cooperation. Lone wolves can be successful, but they can be even more successful if they work with others.

John Hattie and Klaus Zierer (2018)

Dealing with a wider range of colleagues can only add to the complexity of your work. A way to ease the pressure is to make *collaboration* a fundamental part of everything you do. John Hattie and Klaus Zierer (2018: 26) provide strong evidence on this. In *10 Mindframes for Visible Learning*, they state that "collective efficacy" has one of the highest positive impacts on learning (an effect size of 1.23, if you're interested). Talk openly with colleagues from different schools and let them know how highly you value their contributions. By building levels of collaboration, you will have a better chance of success. The middle leader who embraces the system approach is the epitome of a collaboration-driver.

The CPD element

Visiting another school in your network to carry out lesson observations or do a more informal learning walk could be one of your tasks. These are probably the most straightforward elements. It is likely that there will be an agreed strategy in place for this type of work. How you feed back is essentially the same as with the team in your school.

More challenging, for a lot of us, is having to deliver CPD training. This is probably the highest profile aspect of your system-wide role, as you will be seen and judged by colleagues in other schools. We won't spend time here discussing how to deliver training, but it is something that you will need to think about. Books such as *Presentation Zen* by Garr Reynolds (2012) will help you think about fresh approaches to training groups of adults. Although you might not agree with everything Reynolds says, it will sharpen your appreciation of different techniques.

Teachers can be demanding delegates, and delivering training to groups of them is challenging and can cause a lot of worry. For example, there are some teachers who will expect you to deliver your training in the same way as they are expected to teach their class.

Case study

"This consultant rolled up and, to be honest, if I taught my class the same way he taught us, Ofsted would fail me on the spot!"

Lizzy, Year 5 teacher

Lizzy's comment is one that I've heard so many times. I can see where she's coming from, but she is missing an important point. She assumes that if something works for a group of 9- and 10-year-olds, it will work for a group of 23- to 60-year-olds. But there is a difference. In fact, they are two different types of teaching and learning:

- **Pedagogy:** The *Oxford English Dictionary* definition is: "The method and practice of teaching, especially as an academic subject or theoretical concept."[1]

- **Andragogy:** Refers to teaching concepts that relate to adult learning, which can vary from those used in primary and secondary schools.[2] I think the important difference is that andragogy is less about the academic and theoretical and more about the application of experience.

---

1 See https://www.lexico.com/en/definition/pedagogy.
2 See https://www.lexico.com/en/definition/andragogy.

In Lizzy's comment, we sense a lack of appreciation about the context of the learning. Have a look at Malcolm Knowles' (1984) four principles of andragogy. These points are quoted from a precis of his work:

1. *Since adults are self-directed, they should have a say in the content and process of their learning.*

2. *Because adults have so much experience to draw from, their learning should focus on adding to what they have already learned in the past.*

3. *Since adults are looking for practical learning, content should focus on issues related to their work or personal life.*

4. *Additionally, learning should be centred on solving problems instead of memorizing content.*[3]

Stephen Pew (2007: 17) draws our attention to Marcia Conner's (n.d.) five components of andragogy, which include telling adult learners why the work is important and showing learners "how to direct themselves through information". Significantly, "people will not learn until they are ready and motivated to learn".

Before you deliver your CPD material, tell your group how you will be presenting the content and why you've chosen to do it this way. Use the points we've discussed relating to how adults learn to outline your approach. That way you will avoid any misunderstanding. I think it is clear which ones relate to adding value.

Tell them:

- What you are going to cover – the content.

- How you are going to deliver it – the process.

- What's in it for them – the benefits.

By making it clear that this is an adult learning setting, your group won't expect some sort of "Ofsted lesson", but rather one catered for them specifically.

Without doubt, some learning strategies do fit across different settings. I have always found that allowing delegates to discuss things amongst themselves is very effective. The trick is to not overdo it or make it feel like a replica of a school lesson.

---

3 See https://www.learning-theories.com/andragogy-adult-learning-theory-knowles.html.

Monitoring the training you provide – don't make the same mistakes twice

Regardless of how you decide to run your training session, it is important to know how it went.

Case study

"The training we had with the teacher [from another school in the MAT] didn't cost much. And you could tell!"

Fiona, secondary maths teacher

Lower cost is an advantage of providing in-house CPD. However, colleagues will not sit by and happily accept a day of poor INSET. It won't matter that you are saving the school money; you still have to provide value. Honest evaluation of your work will help you identify which aspects your colleagues appreciate, and you can build on these.

You will, most likely, have filled in many evaluation forms and become familiar with their formats. There is nothing wrong with adapting these for your own use. Where some evaluations fall short is in only providing a snapshot of how your colleagues feel at the end of a training day or sequence. This doesn't reflect how much impact the training will have. I can remember a training session in which we were taught to juggle. The end-of-day evaluations were good, because we had fun, but in all honesty, the juggling was the most memorable part and I can't remember changing my practice because of the training content.

A more effective evaluation design is to give people the chance to evaluate immediately after the event *and* at later dates. The appropriate frequency is for you to decide, perhaps after a month or half term, and then at the end of term and a year later. By adding a series of evaluations, you will get a better idea about the sustainable impact, and it will help colleagues to keep their focus on the changes. Tell your colleagues about this at the start of the training. This sends the powerful message that you are in this for the long term and that their opinion will be continually sought. This process will communicate your professionalism to your colleagues. You will be showing how you value their long-term input, and this will enhance the value of your training sessions. Immediate feedback will have more relevance if it can show a before-and-after picture. Try doing a skills audit before the training starts so that delegates can see how far the training has taken them at the end of the day.

An example: you are a phase leader and want to increase the effectiveness of TAs across the classes in your remit. You have been on a course related to this, and you have concluded that it's vital to get teachers and TAs talking to each other.

You run a day of training. The key objective for the day is to increase both teachers' and TAs' ability to:

- Talk to each other more often.
- Have meaningful conversations about the learning in their classes.
- Feel more comfortable discussing difficult issues.
- Have the confidence to talk openly about professional issues.
- Be better at listening to what others are saying.
- Appreciate the views of other professionals.

At the beginning of the training, ask the attendees to fill out a form that sets the objectives out as statements, to which they offer graded responses.

An example:

"I have the confidence to talk openly about professional issues."

Not at all	To a limited extent	To some extent	To a considerable extent	To a great extent

Repeat this at the end of the training. You might like to do this before and after each section, if your training day is broken down into different components. This helps delegates to reflect on the last topic before moving on to the next. Use your professional judgement here. Too many stops and starts to fill out forms can spoil the flow of your training, so apply as you see fit. I have seen this work well when used before and straight after natural breaks. Do as you see fit on the day.

Along with later evaluation, it is worth adding another layer to enable you to judge impact. This can either be done in written format or, more powerfully, as an interview with some or all of the colleagues involved. Obviously, this has time and budget implications, but if it's worth doing, it needs to be done properly. It also sends the message that feedback is not just an admin exercise, but something you care about.

You can avoid additional cost and time by using video call or conferencing software. However, there are times when you can't beat a face-to-face conversation. There is so much you can get from body language.

I've compiled some questions from the hundreds of questionnaires, evaluation sheets and interviews I've had over the years. None are particularly original, but it's always helpful to have a starting point. Feel free to adapt as you wish.

- Which part of the training worked best for you?
- What worked the least well?
- Were there any activities that got to the point better than others?
- What changes will you be making because of the training? This can be both to your own practice and to the school's.
- What messages will you be taking to your senior leaders?
- How will you pass the content on to anyone who couldn't make it?
- How would you like me to follow up the training?
- What, in particular, do you need from future training?

Another approach takes inspiration from the text messages I get after I've accessed my phone company's helpline. Write some statements about different aspects of the training and ask your colleagues to give it a score from 1 (not at all helpful) to 5 (very helpful). For example:

- How useful was the video clip of the English lesson in relation to pupil dialogue?
- How relevant to you was the paired discussion about break-time behaviour in Key Stage 4?

This method is quick and easy.

Proof that you are interested

Evaluating your contribution is very important. It is worth designing an evaluation plan and then sharing it with your led colleagues. By telling people what is being evaluated and when the evaluation points are, you are helping them to understand the whole process and its benefits. Having an open dialogue with your team about the evaluation plan will help you to identify their expectations and how well these have been met.

Honest reflection

Have you ever had real proof that action has been taken due to an evaluation form that you've filled in?

If you have:

■ What was the action?

■ How did it make you feel about the trainer and whether you'd be happy to work with them again?

If not:

■ What were you expecting?

■ Did it help you form an opinion of the trainer?

■ Did it make you doubt the use of evaluations?

Reflecting on this will help you to consider how you use evaluations to inform your future practice, as well as influencing how others might view you.

Concluding thoughts

System leadership opens up a whole new sphere of influence for middle leaders. Use this opportunity to sharpen your leadership skills ready for senior roles later in your career.

Honest reflection

With this knowledge, to what extent are you likely to change your practice?

What might you:

■ stop doing?

- start doing?
- continue doing?

With this knowledge, to what extent are you likely to encourage others to change their practice?

What might you ask others to:

- stop doing?
- start doing?
- continue doing?

Chapter 7

Dealing with Conflict and Difficult Conversations: Overcoming Awkward Situations

Effective problem solving [...] is a series of courageous conversations, not just a one off. That's why this management stuff is so hard, and ultimately so rewarding.

Larry Reynolds (2015)

By the end of this chapter, you will have an overview of dealing with conflict and difficult conversations, and some recommendations for further reading.

Unfortunately, disagreement amongst people in any workplace is inevitable. This is especially so in people-intensive professions in which there is a lot going on, and schools are perfect examples of this. It means that no matter how civil, empathetic and fair you are, you can expect conflict from time to time.

Honest reflection

How often are you aware of conflict at work? Who is involved and what are the issues?

List the conflicts in categories such as: colleagues versus parents, you versus parents, colleague versus colleague, you versus colleague.

What was the conflict about?

By doing this as an aspiring or new middle leader, you will start to get a detailed picture of where conflict occurs and the type of issues linked to different roles. Ask more experienced colleagues for their reflections based on these questions.

Discuss with SLT colleagues the types of conflict that they encounter. Do they manifest differently in their role?

Use this activity to prepare yourself for the inevitable.

The saying "10% of conflict is due to difference of opinion; 90% is due to tone of voice" is quoted regularly and it could well be true, but it's not as simple as that.

Middle leadership conflict scenarios

There are two common scenarios in which you, as a middle leader, will come across conflict:

1. When someone complains to you about something that is your responsibility.
2. When you need to act as a mediator between two parties.

Whatever the cause, it is important for you to act quickly. Disagreements will lead to a bad working atmosphere, which can impact on the children's learning. This environment must not be allowed to develop. If you tend to shy away from conflict, try not to. If a led colleague or a parent thinks you are ignoring their problem, their trust in you will be lost. Your team expect your support. Make sure they get it by acting swiftly. Parents expect you to have their child's welfare as a priority. Don't give them evidence to suggest anything else.

Although there are many causes of conflict, *lack of information* is a common one. Add to this a tendency for people to believe gossip and hearsay and you have a perfect recipe for misunderstanding that leads to anger and disagreement.

This is why *clarity* is essential. Knowing that, read this case study:

Case study

"I had this member of staff who didn't like me very much. He was great friends with my predecessor and, to be frank, he thought he was untouchable. He'd been in the school for years. When I took over, he didn't like being asked to do anything other than the basics. Anyway, we had an inspection at the time, and the inspectors, four or five of them, were in for four days. On the second day, a parent came in to say that she was taking her daughter to a different school because the girl hated being in this teacher's class. The parent said that several others were thinking about doing the same thing. This is not what you want to hear with inspectors looking over your shoulder all day, every day.

"I knew that Jez would react badly if I told him. At least, I had been told that he often went a bit flaky under pressure. From all accounts, he nearly didn't turn up when the place had been inspected before. I couldn't risk him bailing out, so I kept it to myself. This 'need-to-know' tactic was used by a head with whom I'd worked as a deputy and it seemed to work for him. 'What they don't know can't harm them' was his motto. So I did the same thing.

"The day after the inspection, I was on a training day with our nursery class teacher. We had been given a provisional 'good' rating. That was great for us. I was very relaxed. I didn't think about getting in touch with Jez. I assumed he'd be pleased with the result. It went wrong for me when the child who was leaving told the rest of the class that she was off, and that her mum had cleared it with me. This was during the day that I was out.

"It's fair to say that Jez went mad. He didn't like the fact that I hadn't told him. The school secretary told me how he went around screaming about my incompetence to anyone within 20 yards of him. When I saw him the following day, he'd calmed down a bit but was still fuming. I said that I could understand his feelings. But, and this still annoys me now, I didn't tell him why the child was leaving. He was blissfully unaware that he was so unpopular. I kept that from him. But perhaps I should have got in touch with Jez as soon as the inspection was over."

Pippa, head teacher

Honest reflection

Have you ever been in a situation in which you have found out that information had been kept from you? Perhaps this eventually came to light because:

- Someone else told you whilst events were unfolding.
- You found out after the event.

If "yes", how did that affect your confidence in the leader who withheld things from you?

Is there ever a time when it is right to not tell a colleague something?

- Perhaps it might do unnecessary damage?
- Perhaps they are not entitled to know the information?

Write your thoughts down. Reflect on them.

How would you have dealt with Pippa's situation?

Try talking to a senior leader about this type of thing. Ask them if there are instances when they might withhold information. Consider how you ask this question. It's probably best to ask for general advice rather than push for specifics. Find out how they would have responded if they were in Pippa's shoes.

Dealing with a complaint about you or something you control

A typical conflict scenario is a parent complaining about their child's performance in your subject area or an issue to do with behaviour in the age phase that you lead. Quite often they could be unhappy with the approach of one of your team members and want you to deal with it. Another middle leadership situation is when a team member is unhappy with a performance review or workload issue. They bring their complaints to you and want some kind of resolution. In any of these cases, the person complaining wants to see a result which is in their favour. Ideally, everyone involved will be fully informed at the start of the resolution process, but you can't guarantee that this will be the case. Actually, I would go as far as to suggest that it is extremely unlikely.

Use an established process

When you are in a meeting with an angry party, a good starting point is to *ascertain the facts*. Ask them what they know about the situation. Listen very carefully and make notes. This will let them know that you are taking their complaint seriously and your evidence-gathering will be accurate. Also, the more you focus on logging the details, the better equipped you'll be to ask questions.

Openly making a written record of what is said sends a strong message that it will be referred to later. This encourages people to be as accurate as possible. It is good to check that taking notes is alright with the people involved. Getting their permission makes it clear that you are being transparent about the whole process. Read the notes back to check that the other person agrees with them. Checking what the other person has said and agreeing on it has a miraculous effect on their honesty!

This process will give a good indication of how informed the aggrieved person is. If this identifies some glaring gaps in their knowledge, you can put them right, but you need to be diplomatic. You don't want the aggrieved person to feel that you are belittling them. Sometimes this is enough. They might well have not been aware of all the facts and as soon as they can see the full picture, they accept it. You do get people who still won't concede out of pride, but with the facts against them, their arguments are hollow – and they know it.

We are fooling ourselves if we think resolution is as simple as that in every case. In *Courageous Conversations at Work*, Larry Reynolds (2015: 65) suggests a four-step process for problem solving, which is very applicable to the difficult meetings we might have. Larry's process is called PDA2.

> *P stands for present situation.*
>
> *D stands for desired outcome.*
>
> *The first A is for analysis.*
>
> *The second A is for action.*

When you meet the complainer, you need to agree on where you are at present and where you want to end up. Having sorted that out, you need to unpick the cause of the conflict. Once you agree on this, you can start doing something about it.

When following the PDA2 process, the opening conversation can be as simple as: "Hello. We really need to resolve this issue, as I'm sure you agree. So let's talk about how things are at the moment and decide how we'd like to see things turn out. We need to get to the bottom of all the facts and see how we can put things right."

Have a definite structure prepared

Running through some focused questions should help you see things more clearly. It is very effective to ask the person you are having the discussion with to look through the questions as well. If they can think about them before the meeting, so much the better.

- What are the facts? No assumptions: just the facts.
- In my view, what is the other person claiming? These ideas can be classed as assumptions.
- What do I need to find out?
- What have I done to cause and/or perpetuate this conflict?

- What does the ideal outcome look like?

- What concessions am I willing to make?

If you go to a meeting with some prior thoughts about these questions, it will be easier to get the conversation going. A good place to start will be with both of you being open about the first point. This goes back to what we were saying before – there could be significant misunderstandings on both sides, and this will help to identify them.

A simple tool to use is the assumption matrix:

What I know	What I think I know	What I don't know/ need to find out
There is a long-running dispute between Amrat and Belle about workload.	Amrat does a lot more than Belle, especially when it comes to contributing to curriculum development (a specification in the contract) – at least, this is what he says.	The facts. Does Belle do less work in this situation? If it is the case, why is it? If not, what is causing Amrat's concern?

This is a surprisingly effective tool. If both parties fill it in, it can highlight the differences in what they claim to know. Be prepared for some interesting conversations about what people *think* they know.

Honest reflection

If you have complained to a senior colleague, recall what actions they took during the meeting.

- Did they take notes?

- Did they appear to be listening carefully?

- Did they regularly check what you were saying in order to agree on what your complaint was about?

If you were happy with the meeting, what made that possible? Did you prepare anything beforehand?

Make a note of this and use it yourself with colleagues who come to you with a complaint. If the opposite occurred, remember how this made you feel.

The value of being assertive

Being assertive will help you through the meeting and it is something a good leader needs to perfect. It might not come naturally to you, but perfecting it will be very worthwhile. I had to learn it. I feel like I am flicking a switch into "assertive mode", but it works. This is particularly useful for those of us who tend to avoid conflict or don't like raising difficult questions. Having worked for several pleasant leaders who had their "niceness" exploited, I can see the value of this skill.

Assertive is not the same as aggressive, which, sadly, is something that a lot of people tell me their leaders can be. It's about putting your opinions forward in a way that is honest and straightforward. You need to be able to stand up for your views whilst respecting the other party's take on things. It is good to understand that whilst you have a point to make, so does the other person. You both want to come to a good conclusion, even though the desired outcome may be different.

There are some golden rules that will help you keep control and guide the difficult conversation. Ken and Kate Back (2005) have some very useful work on this in the excellent *Assertiveness at Work*.

▨ Be specific about the points you are making and take things step by step.

▨ Do not get personal. Only focus on the problem.

▨ Ask for the other person's views and react to them calmly.

▨ Ask for the other person's solutions.

▨ Talk about how you can both contribute to the conclusion.

▨ Draw up the actions you agree on.[1]

---

1 List adapted from Back and Back's (2005: 122) flow diagram.

Choose your words carefully

The right words have a profound effect. When clarifying things, ask:

- How do you see things?
- What, do you think, caused this to happen?
- I want to make sure I've got this right. Is this how you see it?
- What changes can we make?
- So, let's agree that …

Honest reflection

Has there been a time when you've gone to a senior colleague with a complaint and come away feeling harshly treated?

- Did you feel that they were listening to you?
- Were you allowed to explain your points in detail?
- Were you allowed to suggest a way forward?
- Did the person you were complaining to seem to want to win regardless of any evidence?

Think about this. It will help you know how to behave when a colleague comes to you with a complaint. They might be in the wrong, but sending them away feeling upset and angry will not help to build a good team relationship.

It is not about "giving in", but "putting them right" in a professional way. Asking the right questions will help build trust.

The values clash dilemma

A tricky area of conflict comes when you have to enforce something that doesn't fit your values. A good strategy here is to let the aggrieved person know that you understand how they feel and that you share some of their anger or frustration. Use your *empathy* disposition.

Don't say, "I'm only the messenger," but agree that things are difficult. If you can persuade them to agree that something does need to change – even if they don't approve of the proposed course of action – then you have some common ground. Understanding that there is a problem and that it needs solving gives you the opportunity to involve the aggrieved person. Find out what they would do. If your team member can see that you share their concerns but are keen to sort things out, this will build trust in your relationship. Be transparent about your situation and allow them to see how you are caught in the middle. This won't be popular with the senior staff who think your role is to support whatever they believe, but I think that it is worth standing your ground.

If the person who's raised the complaint can't see that there is a problem or if the way of solving it is still causing concern, then you are within your rights to say that you will take their thoughts to senior leaders. As a middle leader, I found it useful to say that I'd pass their concerns on confidentially. Again, this can build trust. You will be seen as someone who is there to represent the team and its members.

Senior leaders should be open to comments from everyone in the school. In fact, this is a key part of the middle leader role and comes into play in many industries. As a middle leader, you are the link between the chalkface and non-teaching leaders. Your comments, feedback and insights should be valued by senior colleagues, as it is a way for them to keep in touch with the day-to-day practice of the school. Use this situation to underline the value of your middle leadership role. You are not just an information channel, but a genuine communicator of real-life issues that affect performance. Liaising between your team and senior colleagues will show that you have the whole school as your focus.

Being the mediator between colleagues

If there is conflict between any of your team members, it becomes your conflict as well. It is expected that you solve these issues as part of your role. This is an area that causes a lot of stress and anxiety for any leader. A falling-out between members of your team will have a negative effect on morale and this will damage performance. It is a difficult scenario because you must not be seen to be taking sides. This is a fundamental rule, but it can be hard to carry out, especially if the dispute is between two colleagues with whom you get on well. This is one of the thankless parts of the job.

A good place to start is by having one-to-one conversations with the protagonists. It's good to get a clear picture of what they each think. You can't do this information-gathering effectively at the start of a meeting with both sides sitting opposite each other, especially if emotions are running high, so make sure you talk to them individually first.

Use the preparation structures noted on pages 113–114 and the clarification questions on page 116. It is worth making time to ask your team members to look through the questions so they can come to the one-to-ones prepared. As suggested earlier, identifying the facts, as they see them, will be a good start because the one-to-one meeting could reveal a lack of understanding from one or both sides. This could, again, be down to misinterpretation or missing information. It is not unusual to find both sides in this position. It's worth encouraging everyone to recognise that events can be perceived differently. If you can pinpoint the facts, you will be identifying some common ground, which will help.

It is good to have a policy for conflict meetings, so you can refer both parties to it before you get together. Here are some ground rules for colleagues to look at prior to the meeting:

- Appreciate that other people will see things from a different perspective.
- Understand that this different perspective will have influenced how people think.
- Allow the other person to finish what they are saying and not interrupt.
- Agree that we will start by setting out the facts as each party sees them.
- Agree that all parties will have the chance to suggest what the outcomes should be and will be allowed to give an opinion on how to get there.
- Agree to treat each other with respect, no matter how much we disagree.

Your job is to run an effective team. The less conflict there is, the more productive you will be. If you are known as a leader who can solve conflict, your reputation will be very high.

Giving negative feedback – always a difficult conversation

We all need people who will give us feedback. That's how we improve.

Bill Gates (2013)

If you are giving feedback to a team member who has underperformed in some way, there are times when it is easy. It is never pleasant, but it can be straightforward. For example, if you have just seen a lesson that was clearly below the expected standard, your colleague might be self-aware, in agreement and hoping for some suggestions on how they can improve. Or if you are looking at a planning sheet that is way off the agreed format, you both have the evidence in front of you.

No matter how straightforward the negative feedback is, you still need to consider how it is given, so it is worth referring back to Chapter 2 at this point. Perhaps a degree of empathy is needed. You will not gain anything by being uncivil or unpleasant. I'm not saying that you need to be unrealistically nice, but there is no need to be a spiteful bully.

The hardest feedback to give is when a colleague doesn't accept what you are saying. This tends to happen when there is a degree of subjectivity involved. Lesson observations are examples of this, because you are stating your opinion, not referring to fact. Obviously, there will be times when something is an agreed failure – if the class behaved badly and the teacher made no attempt to address it, you will have evidence of this. But things like the teaching approaches deployed in a lesson can be the source of more nuanced disagreement.

Case study

"I was watched doing a DT lesson. We had cereal boxes that the children had to make into a model of a monster with moving jaws. It was to do with using cams. It was an hour long. At the end, the observer said it was good, but could have been better. I was really disappointed. I thought it had gone very well. He said I should have got them to explore how the jaws would move differently if you put the cams into different places. But I said that was coming next week, and anyway, there wasn't enough time to do that in an hour. He wouldn't have it. I went from being a bit disappointed to getting really mad."

Terri, Year 5 teacher

Terri's example is common. We can have different expectations of lessons and this will inevitably lead to disagreement. Marcus Buckingham and Ashley Goodall (2019) suggest that we're not as reliable at rating other people as we think we are. They say we are too heavily influenced by our own experiences and our own sense of "what good looks like". Good leaders accept this.

I have watched countless lessons and given feedback to hundreds – no exaggeration – of teachers and trainees. I have read books and articles on the subject and have developed a strategy for this challenging part of the job. Here are some points to make it easier:

Advice	Don't say this	Do say this
Don't make it personal.	*You* didn't do that properly.	That part of the lesson could have done with …
Ask for clarification.	The section was poor.	Why did you do that?
Encourage justification. You might have read the situation wrongly.	Well, that was an ineffective thing to do.	What was the outcome? *(Be clear if you have evidence that the strategy didn't work as the colleague thinks it did.)*
Start to look for alternatives.	It would have been better if …	Do you think it might have gone better if … *(giving a suggestion)*
Find some common ground.	That's what we expect – so do it this way.	Can you see why I've pointed that out? Why not try …?
Make sure your points are clear.	Make sure you work this way in future.	What needs clarifying? Is there anything you still don't get?

To defuse a tense situation, use language that shows you are trying to help. This follows Ken and Kate Back's advice of offering your colleague the chance to justify their actions. Suggesting alternatives can also work well because you are providing solutions:

- I can see where you're coming from, but what about …?
- Why not give my suggestion a go? I'll take the blame if it doesn't work.

If a colleague refuses to accept what you say, it often is a case of defensiveness and they do not want to give in. Leave them with a suggestion and let them mull it over. It can be hard keeping calm when someone is refusing to take your advice even though you've made a good point. Getting angry won't make them accept what you're saying. It will only make them less responsive.

Take Donna's advice:

Case study

"I was telling an NQT that just giving the kids who'd finished more of the same work wasn't extending their learning. I suggested that they should be given more challenging tasks and told that they were being rewarded by having more interesting things to do. She didn't want to know. Refused. Looked at me like I didn't have a clue. I could tell she was getting stroppy, so I left it. I said something like, 'Well, give it a try if you fancy it some time.' Two weeks later, a TA told me she'd just had a great lesson because … guess what!"

Donna, lower Key Stage 2 lead

Blunt criticism delivered as a statement of fact can have lasting negative effects. Buckingham and Goodall (2019) show how constantly focusing on negatives causes the brain to close down its learning areas, and this slows our ability to take on new information. They add to this by proposing that you can't become excellent by studying failure. This raises the question about how we should be addressing areas that need improving. Surely we shouldn't just ignore them? Buckingham and Goodall suggest helping the colleague to think about how they have dealt with similar problems in the past and how they could apply that to this new situation. Asking the question, "What actions do you need to take?" will pass the responsibility to your led colleague and give them ownership.

Make sure that your team understand the process

Most schools have a feedback policy relating to performance management. Make sure you read it. They are usually strong on how to give feedback but guidelines on how to receive it aren't as common. Your team needs to understand that if comments are negative, they should try not to be defensive and argumentative. Led colleagues should be confident that if they receive criticism, they will be encouraged to put their view forward and that they will also get suggestions for improvement. They should trust that your aim is to give feedback which is constructive – but that's for you to convey.

One last word. If you find that things are getting too hard for you to handle, never worry about getting help from senior colleagues: it is what they are there for.

Concluding thoughts

The more senior your leadership position, the more likely you are to have to deal with conflict. If you find yourself having to have a difficult conversation, don't avoid it or pass it up the ladder too quickly. Try and have a go yourself. Prepare yourself and take action. It will be invaluable practice.

Honest reflection

With this knowledge, to what extent are you likely to change your practice?

What might you:

- stop doing?
- start doing?
- continue doing?

Chapter 8

Productivity: At the Heart of Leader-Teacher Workload

And always bring 100 per cent of your attention and mental resources to bear on high-priority tasks.

Jan Mühlfeit and Melina Costi (2017)

By the end of this chapter, you will have an understanding of how to be productive in a middle leadership role in order to be effective as both a leader and a teacher.

When you are a full-time class teacher, you have minimal control over how to organise your day. Lessons, marking, preparation, meetings: the timings are done for you. The demands on you change when you take on a middle leadership position, as you will appreciate having read Chapter 5. Although in some larger secondary schools some have little or no classroom commitment, many middle leaders will have a heavy teaching load. However, it's likely that you can expect more non-teaching time than the average class teacher. It is what you do in that out-of-classroom time that you'll have more control over. This can be harder than you think. For a start, you don't have the security of someone telling you exactly what to do and when to do it during these times.

A whole industry has built up around time management. This has developed into important work on productivity, which is worth exploring as a middle leader, especially in terms of considering how to use your dedicated leadership time. In this chapter, we haven't got the space for an in-depth look at productivity, or the products its industry is developing, but I do have some recommendations for online tools:

Asana: https://app.asana.com/

Ayoa: https://www.ayoa.com/

Evernote: https://evernote.com/

Trello: https://trello.com/

Wrike: https://www.wrike.com/

Take the time to find productivity and project management tools that suit your way of working.

The real-life challenges of middle leadership

As we've seen, this is a job in which you find yourself right in the middle of things. You will get emails from those above you and from colleagues who you lead. You could get phone calls from parents and demands from governors. It can seem like never-ending demands on your time. One problem is making sure that the work generated by your teaching doesn't take too much time away from your leadership duties – and, of course, vice versa. This is common in the education world and people in this position often find that they end up doing neither particularly well.

There was a time when our pigeonholes would have four photocopied sheets sticking out of them in the morning, and that was the day's work. Not anymore. Those days have long gone. We now have technology that keeps us informed and reminded with alerts and emails arriving every minute. Add to this the velocity of school life and you can see how we can be overwhelmed and our productivity diminished.

A common mistake that new middle leaders make is trying to do too much. We want to make an impression and, hey, we've got all this non-teaching time! No matter what advice is given, a lot of us find it difficult to say "no" when we're newly appointed and so we take on more and more. It might be manageable for a while, but the overload will soon strike. Because it's very difficult to ask colleagues to take work off you after you've made a point of taking it on, you keep struggling with it. Try to avoid this from the start by managing what you offer to be involved in.

You should also be aware of the macho, and masochistic, "Look at me, I'm so busy!" competition. Unfortunately, there are leaders out there who like to judge people on how early they arrive in school and how late they leave. Try to not get caught up in this. A quick comment here: if you can't avoid this because of the culture of your school, do not arrive early *and* stay late *and* take a lot of work home.

Although – as we'll see shortly – the traditional to-do list might be inappropriate in our modern schools, you'll need a list of some description. This will help you to prioritise, and this is very important. As a middle leader, you will find yourself having to spin a lot of plates. You will need to develop your prioritising skills.

This is a common scenario:

- You have to write a new scheme of work for your subject area/or a new policy for reporting to parents in your age phase that reflects whole-school policy but is relevant to the age of the children. You have two weeks to come up with a draft for the SLT to evaluate.

- You teach two lessons on Monday.

- You spend Sunday preparing them.

- One lesson is at 9.40 a.m., the other 2.15 p.m.

- First thing in the morning you find out that someone in your department/age phase is off sick.

- Cover needs to be arranged. At the moment, it is your responsibility to let the admin staff know.

- Another colleague sent an email late last night to complain about the resources on the school system. This needs to be sorted as soon as possible.

- In-between your lessons you have to watch two colleagues teach. The school policy is for feedback to be given after school on the same day.

- During lunchtime you check your school email. There are 15 new messages. Some are specifically to you from senior staff, some are general school items and one is from a led colleague. This one is flagged "urgent and confidential".

- On Tuesday and Wednesday, you have a full teaching timetable, with a staff meeting after school on Wednesday as well.

- On Friday, you are going to a partner school to deliver some training to colleagues from the same department/age phase.

It's quite easy to see how this can become a mess. It could end up with you taking home piles of marking and planning, along with the training preparation for Friday. The email from your colleague will have added to your anxiety because of the "urgent and confidential" label. The email from the senior leader could be to ask you to go to a conference on Saturday. You are worried because you have only given your leadership tasks brief consideration.

This scenario might be just about manageable if all you had to do was fight these fires. But as we know, school life isn't as simple as that.

Many of your responsibilities will be easy to put in the diary and do without interruption or consideration – for example, lesson observations and subsequent feedback meetings. There won't be much that will take your attention away from these tasks. But there will be times when you will *have to* concentrate on a new development or solve a problem. You will need uninterrupted time to think. This is where productivity advice is valuable.

Case study

"We take them swimming on Thursdays – leave school at 2.15 p.m. The head came with us one day. She sat next to me on the coach and said, 'I don't know what I've done today. One of those days where I do nothing.' Well, I can tell you, as a class teacher, I wasn't very impressed. I spent every day going flat out … not 'doing nothing'. Then I got promoted to lead a key stage and had two days out of the class. Then I got what she meant. I'd often find myself getting to the end of my non-teaching time and thinking, 'What happened then?' I had nothing to show for it! Two days faffing around."

Karen, Key Stage 2 lead

It is worth doing a time audit of your designated leadership time. One way is to log the disruptions.

This is an example of a middle leader with an hour to spend devising a much-needed new planning format.

Disruption: who and what	How long	My reaction/response
Principal's PA dropped in to ask if I had finished the draft policy. Had a chat about the holidays.	Five minutes	Had to be polite, so chatted for longer than I would have hoped. He wouldn't get the hint! Took my mind off the planning format.
Phone notified email from Rick's father. Read it. He's very annoyed about the detention and demanded an appointment.	Two minutes to read it. About another five minutes thinking about what to do.	Had only just got my focus back after principal's PA's visit. Completely threw me off the task.

This is an important part of your approach to your job. Productivity can be the difference between being a reasonably good leader and a very good one. Colleagues will have more trust in a leader who is in control of their work rather than one who is constantly flustered and frantically bouncing from one task to another. We know that leadership is about moving things forward, but by spending your time reacting to things, you aren't really leading. You are being led by circumstance.

Battles for middle leaders' time

Keeping on top of new initiatives in your area is a basic part of your role. Coming up with new ideas about teaching content and ways of delivering lessons is an important part of a middle leader's brief. If your leadership position is more about general school initiatives and practice, you will be devising new strategies and procedures along with monitoring their impact and writing evaluation reports. All this takes time and concentration.

Consider these steps to help you feel more in control of your workload.

On an ongoing basis

A lot of productivity experts in industry talk of the "brain dump". This is a space where you make a note of issues as they arise. This is nothing new, but worth mentioning because it is a useful strategy. Write comments in a notepad or on your phone using something like your reminders app or Evernote. I find that voice recording is good for this. What you are doing here is moving distractions out of your immediate view. It will help you to relax about the flood of new information that is coming your way. You know that nothing will be forgotten. When a colleague catches you in the corridor or on the way out for a break duty to ask you something, this strategy helps to avoid the "Tell me later, because I'll forget" response.

Have a clear plan. This will look like a to-do list, but might be one of the many different variations. I am drawn to Graham Allcott's (2014) *How to Be a Productivity Ninja*, in which he suggests that the to-do list has its limitations. He is right when he says that in an environment where things happen very quickly, priorities can soon be in disarray. There are few places more fast-paced than schools, so have a look at what he has written. Having said that, it is important to know what to put into your plan. It doesn't matter which method you use to manage your productivity, but you must have an idea of your priorities.

A very well-established and simple tool for identifying priorities is the Eisenhower Matrix.

1. Important and urgent

These are the obvious items that must go to the top of the list and stay there until completed. This is likely to be as the result of a poor inspection, a sudden change in legislation or a safeguarding issue. Often, these are things that senior leaders have asked you to do. As the matrix suggests, get on and do it.

2. Important but not urgent

These tasks are things like writing new policies, introducing different ways of teaching, looking into new behaviour management strategies and the like. They are likely to be changes that you feel need to be made to improve your team's performance, but they don't need to be done immediately.

The danger here is that the lack of initial urgency can lead to things being left undone because of the firefighting activities that we get drawn into. It is important to give yourself the time to get on with these projects so that they don't suddenly become urgent. Although quite tricky to achieve, try to build in some slippage time. In reality, you could get called upon to work on an important-urgent priority with little warning. As the matrix suggests, plan this into your work schedule.

3. Not important but urgent

This is a troublesome category and it is where a lot of time gets wasted because of interruptions – for example, a colleague demanding some of your time with: "Can I speak to you for five minutes?" They will feel that their issue needs to be dealt with as soon as possible, and you are bound to ask what it's about. Obviously, if it is something of great importance that needs to be an important-urgent task, then you will deal with it, but often it is the *seeing you* aspect that has the urgency, not the topic being discussed.

One way of addressing this is to have a policy of setting time aside for these conversations. Sara's example is a good one.

Case study

"One of the first things that the new head teacher did was set a time for one-to-one discussions with all the middle and senior leaders – about once every couple of weeks. This meant that we knew there would be a chance to have a chat about things. All of us subject heads thought this was a pretty good idea, so we did the same for each of our team members. It works really well. I don't feel like I'm being hunted down anymore!"

Sara, humanities lead tutor

As Sara's colleagues know that they will be able to bring up important issues at their next meeting, she is not constantly interrupted by team members demanding some of her time.

See if there are any tasks in this quadrant which you could delegate. Do this where possible – but remember that, unlike senior leaders, middle leaders have a limited pool of colleagues to whom they can delegate.

4. Not important and not urgent

It is easy to categorise these tasks as "pointless": something to avoid or "eliminate". In a hard-headed way, this is true, but here we'll also encounter things that can be interesting, fun or engaging – such as the distractions that you find on the internet … and I'm only thinking of work-related items here. However, it is important to keep these off your priorities list.

You might already use this technique or something similar. If you don't, then think of all the things you have to do at the moment and categorise them as I have done in the example table that follows. If you do use this approach, recall all the things that regularly happen or might happen and put them in the table. Consider what type of unplanned event you would have to deal with immediately, which would push other things down your priority list.

Event	Priority	Type of issue/ comments
Daisy wanted to see me immediately because she was concerned about how to write an aspect of the reports to parents.	Important-not urgent	Administration. Daisy is concerned and that is important. Reports not due to be started for three weeks.
Year 5 teacher reports that a child has come into school with cigarette burns on her forearm.	Important-urgent	Safeguarding. Immediate response needed.

A worthwhile task is to work with some colleagues to draw up a list of things that typically happen in school. Use your combined experience to group events that might crop up under different categories. Anything that involves child welfare should be important-urgent. This will prepare you for any eventualities, so that you can respond appropriately.

Knowing how and what to prioritise will also help you to prepare for the "inbox activities" that are a part of some interviews. This task usually presents candidates with a list of scenarios that have to be put in order of priority. It usually starts with: "You arrive at school at 7.30 a.m. to find that …" followed by a list of disastrous scenarios and some less important events. If you are used to this type of activity, this part of the interview process will not be difficult.

Working on a specific project

When you have found a space in your diary to work on an important project, it is very important that it gets your full attention. This is challenging, but I do have some tips to help:

- Investigate the Pomodoro Technique, which was devised in the late 1980s by Francesco Cirillo (2018). Set 25 minutes on your phone timer and concentrate 100% on the task. When the alarm goes, give yourself a five-minute break. As Cirillo says, you can avoid most disruptions for 25 minutes.

- Make sure you have everything you need for uninterrupted work. Things like folders of work for evidence or memory sticks containing important documents need to be to hand. Even though most of your data is stored digitally on the school system, you'll still need to make sure you have easy access to it. If you have to walk around the school to gather bits and pieces as you go, then the likelihood is that you'll be nabbed by someone. "Have you got a minute?" can turn into half an hour, and your momentum is lost.

- Get the tough stuff out of the way. Graham Allcott (2014: 327) talks about the "big rocks" and doing the "worst first". If there's something troubling you, deal with it early. This will clear your mind and help you concentrate. Getting in touch with a parent about a bullying issue or thinking about what to say to a colleague who is underperforming are typical concerns that will put you off getting down to other things. Try to sort them out as soon as you can.

- Olivia Valdes (2018) suggests that if you can see a task that will only take a couple of minutes, do it and cross it off the list. Short, quick wins can be motivating.

- Plan what you are setting out to do and set yourself a target. "Get the final draft scheme of work written within an hour." Achieve that and reward yourself.

- Stick to your prioritised list. Don't drift off into less important firefighting tasks unless they are urgent. For example, inviting Daisy to come into your office for a half-hour tutorial on report writing won't get that scheme of work written.

- Be realistic about having an open-door policy. It is understandable if colleagues interpret your offer of "my door is always open" as an invitation to call by at any time. Set sensible limits.

Honest reflection

How do senior leaders react when you drop by their offices and ask to see them immediately?

- Do they welcome you in?

- Do they ask you to make an appointment for later?

- Do they ask you what it's about first?

- Are you encouraged to come by any time you need?

- Or are you discouraged from doing this?

- Is there an agreed system for meeting senior colleagues at your school?

- Have you ever felt that a senior colleague isn't interested in what's on your mind?

- How could they have done things differently to make you feel less rejected?

Carefully consider these points in order to build up a picture of good practice that you can use.

When you manage to get that time locked into your diary, you need to use a deep work strategy as suggested by Cal Newport (2016). It is essential to give yourself time to think. In *Triple Overload – And What You Can Do About It*, Beat Bühlmann and Graham Allcott (2018: 6) cite research by Kermit Pattison (2008) and Paul Hemp (2009), who found that "knowledge workers" (which is what you are in this part of your job) can spend as much as 80% of their time communicating and collaborating with others. In turn, this leads to interruptions or task switching every 3–5 minutes. If this happens to you when you are working on a key project, you are not likely to get much done. The result? You end up taking more work home.

Do as much as you can to set aside two hours of solid concentration, perhaps using the Pomodoro Technique. This will make you more productive. You will have something to show for your efforts and it is likely to be very good quality. It might not be the finished product, but a well-constructed plan. That work is worth doing. As Bühlmann and Allcott (2018: 10) say: "Experiencing meaningful completion, even of small tasks, creates in us the desire for more completion."

This sounds fine in theory, but school life can provide endless barriers. What if you don't have the office space in which to work without interruptions? Some heads of department will have an office, but others won't. It is unlikely for middle leaders in primary schools to have a dedicated space and I know many secondary subject heads who share an office. You need to find a way around this. See if it is possible to spend time working off-site for an hour or two a week. You might have to pitch the idea well, but it will be worth it. After all, it is not unknown for class teachers to be granted time to write reports at home, so why not allow middle leaders who are without a dedicated workspace the same privilege?

Be wary of the "simple solution"

There is an assumption that major pieces of work can be done in the holidays. With no teaching commitments or interruptions from colleagues, this is an obvious time to set to work on big projects. However, it is not that straightforward. There will be things that you want to develop that won't wait another eight weeks, or however long, until the next break. It is likely that anything which is that important will need input from colleagues, and you cannot expect them to be available at the same time as you during a holiday. It is best to plan your projects so that tasks such as writing up final reports or proposals are scheduled for the holidays. Anything that needs collaboration should be done when everyone is in school. To be honest, when it gets to a break, I tend to shut down completely and find it really hard to get going on school projects. My best work is completed during term time.

Concluding thoughts

Give yourself time to do meaningful work. Ensure you have the time and space to make progress. If you allow yourself to be knocked off this course, your work will be inferior, and you'll end up with stress levels that will only make matters worse.

Honest reflection

With this knowledge, to what extent are you likely to change your practice?

What might you:

■ stop doing?

■ start doing?

- continue doing?

With this knowledge, to what extent are you likely to encourage others to change their practice?

What might you ask others to:

- stop doing?
- start doing?
- continue doing?

Chapter 9

The Next Steps: What to Consider When Moving Up the Ladder

We all need to figure out what tools we have in our toolbox and learn to use them in the right way.

Jan Mühlfeit, and Melina Costi (2017)

By the end of this chapter, you will have a good idea of how to plan for your next career move.

Do your research

A lot of middle leaders are very happy with their position in the school. The job suits them perfectly – some teaching, some leadership and management duties. If you are in that category, then think carefully before considering a move into senior leadership. Some people stay as middle leaders for a long time, even until they retire. As the pressures of senior leadership become more apparent, this is getting more common. These middle leaders are valuable assets to the school. They add stability and their experience has huge advantages. They are often extremely loyal. Although there has been a drop in applications for headship in some areas – as reported by Bethan Lewis (2017) – there are, thankfully, also middle leaders who want to move up to senior positions.

I was in both camps. A deputy head for ten years, I was very happy and not interested in headship. Then things changed almost overnight and I wanted to move on. And I am very pleased that I did. Whichever category you are in, it is worth having a clear understanding of what informs your choice. By going through a process of analysing your thoughts, you will either change your mind or be even more convinced that your decision is the right one for you at the time.

If you think that you want to move up, gather as much information as you can about the next level before applying for jobs. Senior colleagues are the obvious people to ask. Don't just talk to the ones in your school, MAT, alliance or federation; look outside as well. Get as broad a view as you can. Be prepared for warnings and horror stories. It is common in most professions to have a significant number of negative people who will try to deter anyone from taking on the role that they have. In fact, think about how you would describe your role to someone who was thinking about applying for it. Would it be all positive? Even people who love what they do will be able to mention things that could be better.

Motivational speaker Jim Rohn (writing with Chris Widener, 2010) believes that if you surround yourself with people who are positive about their jobs, you will be too. This implies that if you only seek out the negative ones, you will become just like them. Although this is probably a simplified premise, I certainly recognise the effect that groups of negative colleagues can have, and I am fortunate to have worked with some inspirational colleagues with very positive attitudes. If you work with successful, content leaders whenever you can and do things like join social media groups that are positive and supportive, you are likely to be positive too. This stage of your career is where you have a good deal of control over what happens next. You can stay or move on. No one else can make that final decision for you.

Know yourself and know the job

It is always good to have a clear idea of yourself and how well you will fit prospective jobs. Although it can be difficult to be brutally honest about your abilities, coming to terms with your limitations sooner rather than later is a positive move. You will be able to pinpoint areas for development.

Case study

"I can easily take an assembly in front of 200 students. I actually enjoy it. But when I had to explain our new marking policy suggestions to three – yes, three – SLT colleagues, I was a total bag of nerves! To start with, I couldn't get a sentence out. I felt like a complete idiot!"

Samantha, assistant head

Go online and find a person specification and job description for two or three SLT posts. Use the details from these and the information about senior roles that you have gained from talking to SLT colleagues to compile a table like the one that follows. Use this template as a starting point, but add specific features relating to the role you are seeking, along with any additional details that colleagues have given.

Work through the statements, reflecting on where you are now.

Current experience reflection activity			
Statement from job description	**Evidence of what I can do**	**Areas for development**	**People to talk to**
Develop the strategic vision of the school, ensuring a high quality of education through its values and ethos.			
Monitor progress towards the achievement of the school's aims and objectives.			
Lead by example, exhibiting robust values and moral purpose, with an explicit focus on providing an excellent education for all students.			
Build positive relationships with all stakeholders.			
Work with outside consultants to market the school in a positive way that reflects its ethos.			
Be proactive in managing the performance of all staff. Develop systems for tackling poor performance and supporting improvement.			

Statement from job description	Evidence of what I can do	Areas for development	People to talk to
Build and maintain contemporary communication channels that inform parents and carers about pupil performance.			
Establish a culture of "open classrooms" as a basis for sharing best practice.			
Collate data from department heads and monitor progress against national benchmarks.			
Develop and maintain systems to ensure equal opportunities legislation is met.			
Safeguard and promote the welfare of children and young people, and follow school policies and the staff code of conduct.			
Be proactive in your own CPD.			
Work with political and financial astuteness.			
Be the named person for media contact.			
Model entrepreneurial and innovative approaches.			

Source: The statements have been taken from several advertisements and also comments made by senior colleagues. They are representative of the general requirements of senior leadership posts. Some job requirements can change quickly due to government initiatives and other external pressures. Look regularly at new job advertisements to keep up to date with current requirements.

Use this table as a working document and update it as soon as any changes occur in your practice.

Build your evidence and use it

As with any promotion you apply for, the selection panel will be looking for relevant experience. This is also true of some leadership qualifications and courses, so start building a portfolio of evidence as soon as you can. For example, any time you run a meeting, set up a CPD event, monitor colleagues' work or deal with a difficult situation, log it. Use something like Evernote, Microsoft OneNote or Google Drive to keep your evidence in clearly marked folders. That way you can quickly provide examples of the leadership and management tasks you have carried out. Performance management meetings with your line managers are a rich source. Use the evidence of how well you've met your targets, especially leadership ones. This will highlight your ability to understand instructions and follow them. No one will be able to argue that you don't have the whole school's progress as your focus.

To balance this, find incidents in which you have acted on your own initiative to solve a problem or come up with a new idea. You don't want to be seen as someone who can only follow orders. Again, try to link this to a whole-school improvement issue. Match what you have done to the job description table on pages 137–138. This is a real confidence builder. When you apply for a job, use the evidence you have against the school's specific criteria to show the selection panel how well-qualified you are.

Knowing that you are well-prepared and can do what the post requires sets you up well for the written application and interview. If you get the job, it goes a long way to solving the imposter syndrome issue that we mentioned before. Don't delay building your evidence. Trying to go back over what you've done and get the documents together isn't difficult, but it is time-consuming and you are likely to miss things if you rush.

Analyse your evidence

An effective way of using your evidence is to apply a SWOT analysis. The examples that follow are linked to the job description table. Look at the comments to see how they fit, then fill in your own SWOT grid, informed by your evidence.

Strengths

■ **What experience do you have?**

List the work you have been doing, along with qualifications and other forms of CPD.

For example: You have worked with your SLT colleagues to formulate the strategic vision.

■ **What sources of input can you draw on?**

Subject associations and leadership support groups are good for keeping up with new and effective ideas.

For example: Leading by example by teaching excellent lessons or showing good behaviour management outside of the classroom. Evidence of inviting colleagues to see you teach encourages the "open classroom" aspect very effectively.

■ **What do senior colleagues see as your strengths?**

Evidence from performance management meetings.

For example: Official comments about how hard you have worked to provide a safe learning environment.

■ **Which of your achievements give you most pride?**

Choose a particularly challenging issue. This is most effective if it is linked directly to issues at the school where you are applying.

For example: If you have tried hard to build positive relationships with all members of the school community, make this clear. This can be things like parent groups and involvement with governors.

■ **What can you offer more of, where some colleagues fall short?**

This is about spotting a gap in the school's current provision.

For example: You might have heard of a reluctance of some similar level colleagues to engage in CPD, so provide evidence of the training you have received.

Weaknesses

Look at these as things you can do something about. There are still some interviewers who like to ask about your weaknesses. A good response is: "X, Y and Z, and this is how I'm going to address them …"

What parts of the proposed job give you most concern?

There will be aspects of a new role that will worry you. These tend to be areas where you lack confidence, rather than where you have not had the opportunity; perhaps they will be things you have avoided up until now.

For example: A larger scale of "financial astuteness" than you have been asked to demonstrate so far.

Suggestion: Ask to work alongside a colleague who has more to do with financial issues than you do. Approaching the business manager will also be worthwhile.

What do other people consider to be your weaker areas?

This will mean talking to colleagues around you, not just looking at your performance management targets by yourself.

For example: "Modelling an entrepreneurial approach" might be something you think you do, but what if some colleagues can't think of an example?

Suggestion: Create a situation in which you can make your work here very obvious, then get some clear feedback – such as comments in an email thread.

What aspects have you simply not had the chance to do, or been expected to do?

Quite often, these will be on a wider strategic level.

For example: Monitoring how far your school has gone towards achieving its overall aims and objectives.

Suggestion: Identify how the department/age phase you are currently leading is responding to whole-school aims and objectives. Write down some ideas about how you can translate that into the wider school. Look for clear actions that you have taken.

Are there any gaps in your training relating to the tasks you will have to carry out?

Evidence that you have been trained in a specific aspect of the proposed job carries a lot of weight. I have found it particularly useful in areas where gaining hands-on experience is proving difficult. Good training provides strong foundations.

For example: Your implementation of performance management systems might be limited to a small number of people and you may not have had to deal with serious underperformance. Look for ways of addressing this.

Suggestion: Look for training, especially of the sort that asks you to log any actions you take, and then analyse them against a set of success criteria. This does not have to be a costly course provided by external trainers, but can be something put on by your MAT, federation or local authority (if they still provide training).

To get the most from this process:

- Be realistic – it's best to face any unpleasant truths as soon as possible.
- Be honest – tell senior colleagues that you have identified these weaknesses and ask what they did to overcome any similar problems.

Opportunities

Use your weaknesses to identify things that you need to develop.

This will only make you stronger. Choose something that takes you out of your comfort zone. Think of a way of conveying this to the selection panel.

For example: You don't like conflict but you know you will have times when difficult conversations are inevitable.

Suggestion: Read as much as you can about how to navigate difficult conversations, such as Larry Reynold's (2015) *Courageous Conversations at Work*. Assertiveness training will be very valuable but there are plenty of books on this which can help too.

Look for approaches/initiatives that are recent and still becoming established, yet which need refining or driving forward.

We expect new colleagues to bring something fresh to the school, so keep up with new initiatives and approaches that you could offer to introduce or apply in an up-to-date way.

For example: System leadership is growing.

Suggestion: Take advantage of this by showing colleagues how to run a good CPD session for several schools and setting up an evaluation process.

Gain insight into the previous post-holder's approach.

Perhaps your new colleagues have mentioned problems that clearly need to be addressed.

For example: The outgoing colleague was known for being unaware of equal opportunities issues.

Suggestion: Make your credentials clear by citing examples of steps you have taken in this area. This might have been appointing an older colleague who was returning to teaching to your team.

Threats

▣ **Any of your weaknesses can become threats if you let them.**

If you can show that you are acting to address these weaknesses by turning them into opportunities, the threat is reduced: it becomes one that you can do something about.

▣ **Sometimes your current job can put up obstacles.**

This could be a senior colleague who is slow or reluctant to offer you the help needed in order to progress. In this case, you will need to discuss your concerns with them.

▣ **You can expect strong competition at the selection stage.**

There's not much you can do about this, but never worry about missing out to a better candidate. All you can do is ask for feedback and identify what made them better in the eyes of the people appointing them. Be prepared to be disappointed and annoyed, but use it as a positive step.

▣ **The internal candidate.**

There is an increasing trend for schools to appoint from within their MAT or federation. This is challenging if you are applying from outside (but very useful if you are on the inside). You need to know the MAT's philosophy and try to highlight similarities that you have and can evidence. Please bear in mind that you shouldn't apply for a job in any workplace that doesn't align with your own values and beliefs.

Performing this analysis will provide key information – it can point out what needs to be done and put problems into perspective.

Formal qualifications?

This is a difficult topic to write about because things can change considerably if and when new government ministers have a different view to the previous incumbents. It is worth talking to colleagues who have completed any of the routes that we explore here to see if they would recommend what they experienced.

Formal qualifications, such as the National Professional Qualification for Senior Leadership (NPQSL) in England, have been gained by a lot of teachers who want to go for promoted posts. They are not an essential requirement (as the NPQH used to be), but some schools will put things like this in the "desired" column of the person specification, if not in the "essential". Those who enrol on these courses often appreciate their practical nature – they are not just a paper exercise. The assessment process is usually based on practical application and is centred around portfolios of evidence.

Another option is a higher degree in educational leadership and management. At present, providers offer MAs or MBAs in this field. This will add a lot to your understanding of wider issues because you will need to read a lot of articles, academic papers and books. This is time-consuming and can raise workload issues, but most of the people with whom I have worked on MA courses relish the challenge. They appreciate the extensive knowledge and understanding that you gain from being widely read. This has been particularly so for colleagues who have only worked in one MAT. Seeing what others are doing with their practice is an eye-opener.

You will find non-accredited courses as well. I've had colleagues who have gone for this route because they didn't feel the need to gain a certificate or to spend time working on written assignments that would be formally assessed, but they still wanted the knowledge. These courses can be very good at providing you with up-to-date technical leadership language and thinking as well as providing a springboard into more formal training.

Your future

The career middle leader: not just a stepping stone, but something substantial

In Chapter 3, we considered how important it is to be "relevant". This can be a challenge if you stay in the same post for a long time, which I know from personal experience. Because there is a lot of rapid change in education, we feel that because we are naturally moving with the times, we can't be standing still. This is true. I've not come across any middle leaders who are still working in exactly the same way as they were ten years ago. Things move on.

However, you will have to be alert to developments that are being made away from your school. You need to be outward-looking. This way you can have professional discussions about changes that other schools are experiencing. These can be in any part of your role: curriculum, assessment, leadership requirements and a host of other things.

Copy and complete the following table, adding as many categories as you can.

In order to stay relevant, I need to address:

Current experience reflection activity			
Area of work	**Reason**	**Action**	**Time/notes**
Curriculum development	Curriculum needs a refresh. Response to new inspection guidance. We have a lot of new staff and this is an opportunity to liven things up.	Look for subject association training. Talk to colleagues from other schools.	Start looking now with the aim of finding something by end of the spring term. Arrange meeting with Deni from Ashgrove Comp. By half term.
Leadership	No training for ten years.	Book place at subject association's summer conference "How to Be a Great Subject Leader" workshop.	Get the go-ahead by the end of this week and book it ASAP.

If you do this, your colleagues will see that you are enthusiastic and proactive about keeping your practice up to date. It is a good idea to report back on what you've done at staff meetings. Let everyone know what you've been up to and that your career is still developing.

Moving up to senior leadership

Have a clear idea of what you need to do before you take the next step. By analysing job descriptions and person specifications, you can plot how you are going to address the areas you need to develop. All you need to do now is add a *time* column to the job description grid that you made, and you'll have a ready-made action plan. Your school might have something similar, so use whatever suits you.

There will be occasions when you are only a couple of skills short of being able to do the whole list. Don't let that put you off applying for a job. Recognise that these are areas to work on and address them. Being upfront about this to prospective employers can put you in a good light because you will be seen as a reflective professional who is good at self-evaluation.

Concluding thoughts

Whether you intend to stay in middle leadership or move on to a more senior role, it is good to have a plan. It will keep you relevant and highlight the actions you need to take in order to progress.

Learn from your experience and compare it to what other successful leaders are doing. Identify the things you need to do in order to apply for promotions with confidence. That way, you'll know for sure that you are suited to the job.

Honest reflection

With this knowledge, what might you:

- start doing?
- continue doing?

Closing Comments

I'd like to end this book by thanking you for taking an interest in being a middle leader in a 21st century school. School leadership is more challenging now than ever, but its rewards can be difficult to measure. Middle leadership can be the most fulfilling phase of your working life, as well as the most frustrating. It is never dull and always demanding. It certainly isn't for everyone, but everyone has a comment to make about it.

The education system needs people like you to take things forward and ensure that all our young people get the opportunities they deserve. You are the link between what our most senior leaders want and how it is delivered in the reality of the classroom. Without you, the whole thing would fall apart.

I wish you the very best of luck and every success in your career.

If you want to keep in touch, use Bill@BillLowe.co.uk at any time.

I can also be found at:

Twitter: @TeacherInforma1

LinkedIn: https://www.linkedin.com/in/bill-lowe-2014/

References

Allcott, G. (2014) *How to Be a Productivity Ninja*. London: Icon Books.

Allen, D. (2015) *Getting Things Done: The Art of Stress-free Productivity*. London: Piatkus.

Amabile, T. and Kramer, S. (2011) *The Progress Principle: Using Small Wins to Ignite Joy, Engagement, and Creativity at Work*. Boston, MA: Harvard Business Review Press.

Australian Institute for Teaching and School Leadership (2017) *Australian Professional Standard for Principals and the Leadership Profiles*. Available at: https://www.aitsl.edu.au/tools-resources/resource/australian-professional-standard-for-principals.

Back, K. and Back, K. (2005) *Assertiveness at Work: A Practical Guide to Handling Awkward Situations*. Maidenhead: McGraw-Hill.

Bilyeu, T. (2018) How to Master Your Dark Side: Robert Greene on Impact Theory [video], *Impact Theory* (18 December). Available at: https://www.youtube.com/watch?v=LjGqpic7pS4.

Buckingham, M. and Goodall, A. (2019) The Feedback Fallacy, *Harvard Business Review* (March–April). Available at: https://hbr.org/2019/03/the-feedback-fallacy.

Bühlmann, B. and Allcott, G. (2018) *Triple Overload – And What You Can Do About It*. Evernote and Think Productive. Available at: https://evernote.com/c/assets/business/whitepapers/triple-overload/evernote_tripleoverloadwhitepaper.pdf.

Chilvers, P. (2016) Big Beasts or Greatest Servants: Developing Executive and System Leadership. Seminar delivered at the Academies Show, NEC, Birmingham (25 November).

Cirillo, F. (2018) *The Pomodoro Technique: The Life-Changing Time-Management System*. London: Virgin Books.

Clarke, P. (2017) What Are Teaching Schools and System Leaders?, *National College for Teaching and Leadership* [blog] (31 July). Available at: https://nctl.blog.gov.uk/2017/07/31/what-are-teaching-schools-and-system-leaders/.

Conner, M. L. (n.d) Andragogy and Pedagogy, *Ageless Learner*. Available at: http://agelesslearner.com/intros/andragogy.html.

Department for Education (2015) *National Standards of Excellence for Headteachers: Departmental Advice for Headteachers, Governing Boards and Aspiring Headteachers*. Ref: DFE-00019-2015. Available at: https://assets.publishing.service.gov.uk/government/uploads/system/uploads/attachment_data/file/396247/National_Standards_of_Excellence_for_Headteachers.pdf.

Edge, K., Descours, K. and Oxley, L. (2017) Generation X Leaders from London, New York and Toronto: Conceptions of Social Identity and the Influence of City-Based Context, *Educational Management, Administration and Leadership* 45(5): 863–883.

Fausset, R. and Blinder, A. (2015) Atlanta School Workers Sentenced in Test Score Cheating Case, *The New York Times* (14 April). Available at: https://www.nytimes.com/2015/04/15/us/atlanta-school-workers-sentenced-in-test-score-cheating-case.html.

Folkman, J. (2015) Top Ranked Leaders Know This Secret: Ask for Feedback, *Forbes* (8 January). Available at: https://www.forbes.com/sites/joefolkman/2015/01/08/top-ranked-leaders-know-this-secret-ask-for-feedback/#42887a293195.

Foster, S. C. (2018) 7 Things Great Leaders Never Say, *Success* (18 April). Available at: https://www.success.com/7-things-great-leaders-never-say/.

Frangos, C. (2018) 3 Transitions Even the Best Leaders Struggle With, *Harvard Business Review* (2 July). Available at: https://hbr.org/2018/07/3-transitions-even-the-best-leaders-struggle-with.

Fritzsche, D. (2017) Der Software-Elefant, der in der Limmat planscht, *Neue Zürcher Zeitung* (28 July). Available at: https://www.nzz.ch/zuerich/evernote-in-zuerich-der-software-elefant-der-in-der-limmat-planscht-ld.1308047.

Fullan, M. (2011) Leading System Level Change. In H. O'Sullivan and J. West-Burnham (eds), *Leading and Managing Schools*. London: Sage, pp. 16–23.

Gates, B. (2013) Teachers Need Real Feedback [video], *Ted.com*. Available at: https://www.ted.com/talks/bill_gates_teachers_need_real_feedback/transcript.

General Teaching Council for Scotland (2012) *The Standards for Leadership and Management: Supporting Leadership and Management Development.* Available at: http://www.gtcs.org.uk/web/files/the-standards/standards-for-leadership-and-management-1212.pdf.

Goldin, K. (2018) Great Leaders Take People Where They Might Not Want to Go, *Forbes* (1 October). Available at: https://www.forbes.com/sites/karagoldin/2018/10/01/great-leaders-take-people-where-they-may-not-want-to-go/#48b2cdd1421b.

Goleman, D. (2004) What Makes a Leader?, *Harvard Business Review* (January). Available at: https://hbr.org/2004/01/what-makes-a-leader.

Hannagan, T. (2007) *Management: Concepts and Practices.* Harlow: Pearson Education.

Hattie, J. (2012) Instructional Leadership [video]. Leaders in Educational Thought: John Hattie 1(2). Available at: https://www.youtube.com/watch?v=9UYGrk1VpcQ.

Hattie, J. and Zierer, K. (2018) *10 Mindframes for Visible Learning: Teaching for Success.* Abingdon and New York: Routledge.

Helm, C. M. (2010) Leadership Dispositions: What Are They and Are They Essential to Good Leadership, *Academic Leadership: The Online Journal* 8(1), article 21. Available at: https://scholars.fhsu.edu/cgi/viewcontent.cgi?article=1380&context=alj.

Hemp, P. (2009) Death by Information Overload, *Harvard Business Review* (September). Available at: https://hbr.org/2009/09/death-by-information-overload.

Hoffman, R., Yeh, C. and Casnocha, B. (2019) Learn from People, not Classes, *Harvard Business Review* (March–April). Available at: https://hbr.org/2019/03/educating-the-next-generation-of-leaders#learn-from-people-not-classes.

Hopkins, D. (2009) *The Emergence of System Leadership.* Nottingham: National College for School Leadership. Available at: http://www.learnersfirst.net/private/wp-content/uploads/Resource-The-Emergence-of-System-Leadership-Hopkins-2009.pdf.

Irvine, P. and Brundrett, M. (2016) Middle Leadership and Its Challenges: A Case Study in the Secondary Independent Sector, *Management in Education* 30(2): 86–92.

Kanter, R. M. (2012) Ten Reasons People Resist Change, *Harvard Business Review* (25 September). Available at: https://hbr.org/2012/09/ten-reasons-people-resist-chang.

Kanter, R. M. (2013) Six Keys to Leading Positive Change [video], *TedxBeaconStreet* (7 January). Available at: https://www.youtube.com/watch?v=owU5aTNPJbs.

Knowles, Malcolm S. and Associates (1984) *Andragogy in Action: Applying Modern Principles of Adult Learning*. San Francisco, CA: Jossey-Bass.

Levin, P. (2004) *Successful Teamwork: For Undergraduates and Taught Postgraduates Working on Group Projects*. Maidenhead: McGraw-Hill Education.

Lewis, B. (2017) School Head Applications Drop Sharply in Wales, *BBC News* (15 December). Available at: https://www.bbc.co.uk/news/uk-wales-42354800.

Long, R. and Danechi, S. (2019) *Off-rolling in English Schools*. Briefing paper no. 08444 (10 May). London: House of Commons Library. Available at: https://researchbriefings.parliament.uk/ResearchBriefing/Summary/CBP-8444.

MacArthur, H. V. (2019) Treating Employees Like Customers: Why It's Your Best Performance Strategy, *Forbes* (16 April). Available at: https://www.forbes.com/sites/hvmacarthur/2019/04/16/treating-employees-like-customers-why-its-your-best-performance-strategy/#4e3730db16ea.

McClimon, T. J. (2018) Four Ps of Leadership, *Forbes* (4 September). Available at: https://www.forbes.com/sites/timothyjmcclimon/2018/09/04/the-four-ps-of-leadership/#32611c94f828.

Maslow, A. H. (1943) A Theory of Human Motivation. *Psychological Review* 50(4): 370–396.

Masterson, R. and Pickton, D. (2014) *Marketing: An Introduction*, 3rd edn. London: Sage.

Matthias, C. (2014) *National College Annual Survey of School and Children's Centre Leaders 2013*. Research Brief, Ref: DFE-RR333. London: National College for Teaching and Leadership. Available at: https://assets.publishing.service.gov.uk/government/uploads/system/uploads/attachment_data/file/367362/nctl-annual-survey-of-school-and-childrens-centre-leaders-2013.pdf.

Maxwell, J. (2013) The 5 Levels of Leadership [video]. Available at: https://www.youtube.com/watch?v=4KqL_1G8JD8.

Moldoveanu, M. and Narayandas, D. (2019) The Future of Leadership Development, *Harvard Business Review* (March–April). Available at: https://hbr.org/2019/03/educating-the-next-generation-of-leaders#the-future-of-leadership-development.

Molinsky, A. (2016) Everyone Suffers from Imposter Syndrome – Here's How to Handle It, *Harvard Business Review* (7 July). Available at: https://hbr.org/2016/07/everyone-suffers-from-imposter-syndrome-heres-how-to-handle-it.

Mühlfeit, J. and Costi, M. (2017) *The Positive Leader: How Energy and Happiness Fuel Top-Performing Teams*. Harlow: Pearson.

Munro, B. (2019) Academy Boss "Ordered Schools to Cheat on SATs Tests", *BBC News* (25 March). Available at: https://www.bbc.co.uk/news/education-47670746.

Newell, M. (2018) 6 Mistakes New Leaders Make and How to Avoid Them, *Partners in Leadership* (28 November). Available at: https://www.partnersinleadership.com/insights-publications/6-mistakes-that-new-leaders-make-and-how-to-avoid-them/.

Newport, C. (2016) *Deep Work: Rules for Focused Success in a Distracted World.* London: Piatkus.

Newton, R. (2010) *The Management Consultant: Mastering the Art of Consultancy.* Harlow: Pearson Education.

Northouse, P. G. (2015) *Introduction to Leadership: Concepts and Practice*, 3rd edn. London: Sage.

Pattison, K. (2008) Worker, Interrupted: The Cost of Task Switching Fast, *The Fast Company* (28 July). Available at: https://www.fastcompany.com/944128/worker-interrupted-cost-task-switching.

Pew, S. (2007) Andragogy and Pedagogy as Foundational Theory for Student Motivation in Higher Education, *InSight: A Journal of Scholarly Teaching* 2(1): 14–25. Available at: https://files.eric.ed.gov/fulltext/EJ864274.pdf.

Porath, C. and Pearson, C. (2013) The Price of Incivility, *Harvard Business Review* (January–February). Available at: https://hbr.org/2013/01/the-price-of-incivility.

Pozin, I. (2014) 16 Leadership Quotes to Inspire you to Greatness, *Forbes* (10 April). Available at: https://www.forbes.com/sites/ilyapozin/2014/04/10/16-leadership-quotes-to-inspire-you-to-greatness/#163654d067ad.

Public Schools of North Carolina (2013) *North Carolina Standards for School Executives.* Available at: http://www.dpi.state.nc.us/docs/district-humanresources/evaluation/standardsadmin.pdf.

Reynolds, G. (2012) *Presentation Zen: Simple Ideas on Presentation Design and Delivery.* Berkeley, CA: New Riders.

Reynolds, L. (2015) *Courageous Conversations at Work: How to Create a High Performing Team Where People Love to Work.* Kibworth Beauchamp: Matador.

Robinson, V. M. J., Bendikson, L. and Hattie, J. (2011) Leadership and Student Outcomes: Are Secondary Schools Unique? In J. Robertson and H. Timperley (eds), *Leadership and Learning.* London: Sage, pp. 131–142.

Rock, D. (2006) *Quiet Leadership: Six Steps to Transforming Performance at Work.* New York: HarperCollins.

Rohn, J. and Widener, C. (2010) *Twelve Pillars.* Dallas, TX: Jim Rohn International and Chris Widener International.

Schneider, A. and Burton, N. (2008) Personal Intelligences: The Fourth Pillar of School Principalship?, *Management in Education* 22(4): 22–30.

Sinek, S. (2016) People Come Before Money [video] (28 July). Available at: https://www.youtube.com/watch?v=3SVqbM9Nw7Q.

Trobe, M. (2016) Leadership in Challenging Times: How to Enable Your School to Thrive. Seminar delivered at the Academies Show, NEC, Birmingham (25 November).

Valdes, O. (2018) 11 Genius Productivity Tips You Haven't Tried, *ThoughtCo* [blog] (9 January). Available at: https://www.thoughtco.com/genius-productivity-tips-4156923.

Veland, T. D. (2012) A Study of Leadership Dispositions of Transformational Leaders in Georgia High School. Doctoral thesis, Georgia Southern University. Available at: https://digitalcommons.georgiasouthern.edu/etd/814.

Weber, S. (2017) Instructional Leadership: Designing a Culture That Supports Student Understanding, *ASCD Inservice* (30 October). Available at: http://inservice.ascd.org/instructional-leadership-designing-a-culture-that-supports-student-understanding/.

Wood, P. (2017) Overcoming the Problem of Embedding Change in Educational Organizations: A Perspective from Normalization Process Theory, *Management in Education* 33(1): 33–38.

Woods, P. A. and Roberts, A. (2018) *Collaborative School Leadership: A Critical Guide.* London: Sage.

Wrike (2018) *Accelerating Change Management: Getting 7 Personalities on Board* [e-book]. Available from: www.wrike.com.

Yukon Department of Education (2011) *An Educational Leadership Framework for Yukon Principals and Vice-Principals.* Available at: http://www.education.gov.yk.ca/pdf/publications/leadership_framework_principals_and_vice_principals.pdf.

The Subject Leader

Steve Garnett edited by Phil Beadle

ISBN: 978-184590796-9

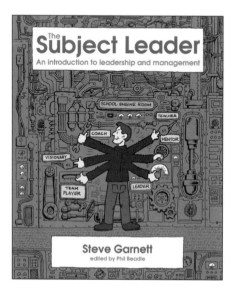

The role of a subject leader is one of the most important in any school, second only to that of the head teacher. Subject leaders are working in the engine room of school life, expected to turn the vision, values and ethos of a school into reality. However, most teachers went into education because they wanted to be teachers, not leaders, so they often haven't had any training into how to lead a subject area.

This book seeks to deliver a whole range of practical solutions to the challenges that the role presents. The areas covered range from setting and communicating your vision, delivering high quality learning across all classes and developing rigorous and effective systems of self-evaluation to understanding and developing a transformational leadership style.

Accessible and realistic, the book also tackles some of the other critical issues that subject leaders might face, such as working with under-performing colleagues and managing the stresses of the role.

The Art of Being a
Brilliant Middle Leader

Gary Toward, Chris Henley and Andy Cope

ISBN: 978-178583023-5

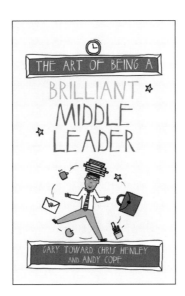

Whether you're already leading or you have it on your radar, this book's for you. Don't expect a textbook full of highfalutin theories though, this book is rammed full of practical ideas that you can use instantly to help you in your current role or to get the position you want. How do you create a brilliant team? What is needed to establish an awesome ethos? How do you do those difficult personnel things? How do you make an impact? Answers to all of these questions and more are based on the combined 70 plus years of the authors' leadership experience in a wide range of educational settings. You'll find a cornucopia of pick and mix tips, strategies and stuff that really works and will make your leadership brilliant!

How to Be an Amazing Middle Leader

Caroline Bentley-Davies

ISBN: 978-184590798-3

Today the myriad skills needed to be an amazing middle leader in schools can seem mind-boggling. What's more, middle leaders are taking up the leadership reins after gaining experience for far fewer years than ever before.

Whether you are new to this role or are more experienced and aspiring to become a school leader, this book will give you the vital information you need in order to understand what is really important about your role and how to improve your key skills. This practical everyday guide covers: the skills of an amazing middle leader; how to inspire others against the backdrop of the busy day-to-day running of a school; effective delegation; leading a team and getting the right things done; developing excellence in your team and sharing good practice; preparation for inspection; and middle leader challenges and next steps.

An outstanding guide for an often neglected group.